Books on Stagecraft

Theory and Craft of the Scenographic Model
Darwin Reid Payne
A precise step-by-step guide to scenic model making
cloth 1193-3, paper 1194-1

Stage Rigging Handbook
Jay O. Glerum
A thorough guide to the safe use and care of stage rigging
comb binding 1318-9

Theatrical Scene Painting
A Lesson Guide
William Pinnell
All the proven techniques of traditional scene painting
paper 1332-4

Sceno-Graphic Techniques
W. Oren Parker
"The original text on theater drafting" in a new, revised edition
paper 1350-2

Third Edition

Sceno-Graphic Techniques

W. Oren Parker

Southern Illinois University Press

Carbondale and Edwardsville

Printed in the United States of America

Edited by Teresa White

Designed by Richard Hendel

Production supervised by Natalia Nadraga

Library of Congress Cataloging-in-Publication Data

Parker, W. Oren (Wilford Oren)

  Sceno-Graphic techniques.

  1. Theaters—Stage setting and scenery—
Drawings.
2. Graphic arts—Technique.　I. Title.
PN2091.S8P34　1987　　792'.025　　86-17859
ISBN 0-8093-1350-2

Contents

Preface

Sceno-Graphic Techniques is the compilation of graphic solutions used in the various stages of planning and executing a setting for the theatre. It seeks to bring together for the special use of the scene designer and stage technician drafting techniques, selected portions of descriptive geometry, pattern making or developments from engineering drawing, and the graphics of perspective. Although the manual is conceived as a *basic* text for the scene designer, it is aimed toward professional levels of drafting and problem solving.

Part One, "The Language of Lines," is concerned with the graphic presentation portion of stage design. It is the study of drafting techniques, conventions, and symbols exceptional to the theatre. Part Two, "Graphic Solutions," deals with the graphic problem solving often needed to draw and make the frequent irregular forms of present-day scene design. Part Three, "Perspective in the Theatre," involves the two forms of perspective: 1) the two-dimensional perspective found in the designer's sketch or representation of a scenic form; 2) the three-dimensional perspective associated with a theatrical illusion or stylistic concept. The first, though used in the theatre to present the designs for a setting, is also found in other disciplines such as architecture and interior design. The second, purely theatrical in origin, examines the graphics of baroque perspective as well as present-day uses.

Grateful acknowledgment is made to Russell McCracken for his assistance in preparing the original text and to Donald Oenslager for his suggestions and illustrative material. Many thanks for their helpful cooperation to Jean and William Eckart, Ned Bowman of Scenographic Media, Willie Hart of T. B. McDonald Construction Company, and to Noel Stanton, technical director, English National Opera, London.

A special thanks for the most helpful and cooperative staff of the Library and Museum of the Performing Arts, Lincoln Center; Beineke Rare Book and Manuscript Library and Yale Theatrical Print Collection, Yale University, in aiding the research of "Perspective in the Theatre."

Sceno-Graphic Techniques was conceived in 1957 at Yale Drama School as a classroom drafting manual. It was the first attempt to organize the drafting techniques of the theatre. In 1964 at Carnegie-Mellon University it was revised and expanded to include part two, "Graphic

Solutions." Since the last edition the interest in the graphics of theatre production has increased. Led by the Graphic Standards Board of the United States Institute of Theatre Technology (USITT), the conventions of technical drafting have been standardized. The technical drafting symbols of this study have been included in this edition along with the new part three, "Perspective in the Theatre."

Part One The Language of Lines

1

Introduction

Any study of the graphic techniques that are practiced in the theatre embraces all phases of technical production, from the designer's vision to the finished set on the stage. A graphic solution, however, is only as accurate as the drafting. It is obvious that a knowledge of drafting techniques is not only the beginning but also the dominating factor in acquiring skill and accuracy at the drawing board.

The most basic use of graphic techniques, in the theatre, is one of communication. Whether it be mounting a production of *Aïda* for the Met, squeezing a set for *Candida* into the Provincetown Playhouse, or designing a twofold for television, the initial problems are the same. Before any scenery gets on the boards, design ideas have to be transcribed into a form that can be easily communicated and understood by others concerned with the production.

There comes a time in the development of any set, simple or complicated, when the designer has to leave the realm of "singing spaces" to come down to earth and deal in feet and inches. As designers they want their ideas carried out efficiently and accurately. To do so, they must give simple, clear and accurate information, the practical information, that is needed to get the set on the stage. Laying aside sketches for the moment, they begin talking in another language, the language of drafting techniques and engineering drawing principles, the language of lines. It is not a language without imagination, however, for it takes considerable visual perception to draw and to read a blueprint.

In the theatre, as in related crafts, the blueprint bridges the gap between the sketch and the completed set on the stage. This period of relative calm may be the calm before the storm when, like a giant jigsaw puzzle, the show is put together. The resulting chaos is not always caused by misinformation but many times by misunderstanding and misinterpretation. At the formative stage of every production it is imperative that everybody concerned understand each other. It is important that everybody speak the same language, a language without visual support of perspective and shading, dependent entirely on lines as its means of communication.

Undoubtedly most designers are familiar with drafting techniques and the principles of engineering drawing. Have patience, the beginning *is* the same but the application is different! The theatre has its own dubious set of drafting conventions, or lack of conventions, that make them worthy of special study. The problems in design, lighting, construction, and movement of scenery are unique to the stage and the allied crafts of television and motion pictures.

2

Tooling Up

Designers or designers-to-be who are turning into draftsmen for the first time, will need to become acquainted with new tools and materials. They will find that drafting skill and accuracy require precision equipment beginning with the working surface, the *drawing board*.

A good drawing board is made of clear white pine, cleated to prevent warping and, for most purposes, about 24″ by 30″ in size.

Are the edges straight? A drawing board is only as good as its edges for if they bow or dip, the T-square will run untrue.

As the preliminary drawings for blueprints are done on tracing paper, the board will need to be padded. Vinyl padding, tinted for just this purpose, provides an excellent drafting surface, protects the drawing board, and saves the eyes by forming a soft contrasting background for pencil lines.

The *T-square*, guiding off the side of the drawing board, establishes the horizontal lines, and its accuracy depends on the straightness of the working edge and the squareness of the head and blade. A 30″ T-square made of hardwood with a transparent-edge blade and fixed head is best for all around service.

Besides establishing the basic horizontal lines, the T-square is the guide for

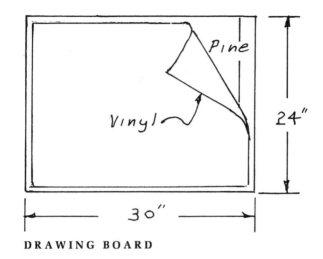

DRAWING BOARD

T-SQUARE

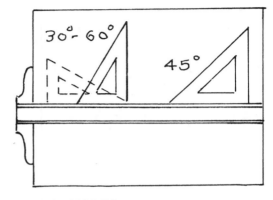 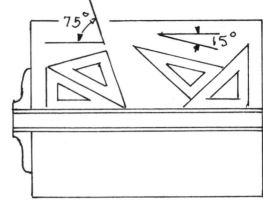 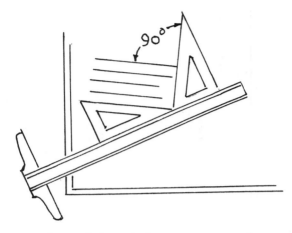

TRIANGLES

triangles. Two transparent celluloid triangles give the customary set of angles. A 6″ 45° triangle and a 8″ or 10″ 30°–60° triangle are the most convenient sizes.

Angles other than the established angles can be drawn by combining the triangles, such as the 45° and the 30°, or the 45° and the 60°.

Odd angles that fall between any possible combinations are drawn by selecting the nearest angle on one of the triangles and placing it on the T-square. The T-square is then slid off the horizontal to reach the desired angle. There are drafting tools designed to assist drawing the odd angles of scenographic drafting. One

is the *set square,* which is a combination triangle and protractor with an adjustable edge that allows the selection of angles between 45° and perpendicular.

The drafting machine, although a more complicated piece of equipment, also provides flexible horizontal and perpendicular straightedges to any part of the board. The edges can be adjusted to any angle that might occur in theatre drafting.

When assembling drawing instruments for the first time, it is wise to invest in the best. The accuracy and clarity of the work depend on the quality of the instruments. Buying a cheap, low-grade set is a nuisance from the beginning and worthless

in a short while. It is better to economize in the number, and obtain a set of good instruments.

The basic drafting instrument is the *compass.* It is necessary to draw a circle or swing an arc. It is quite possible to do a major portion of drafting with a compass as the only instrument. As a matter of fact, the smallest drafting set available is comprised of just a compass with lengthening bar and inking attachments and extra points to turn the compass into dividers.

The lengthening bar is an attachment that increases the length of one of the compass arms and makes it possible to swing

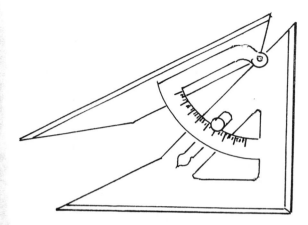

SET SQUARE

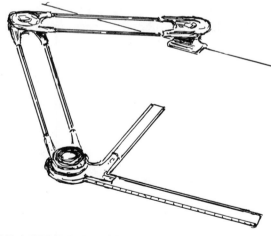

DRAFTING MACHINE

a larger radius arc or circle. The subtle curve of a large radius arc frequently occurs in a show-portal or platform design. Of course, there is time lost changing attachments and most draftsmen would prefer to have a more complete set.

Dividers are used to hold or transfer a dimension. The compass can perform the same operation but with less accuracy. A set containing a 4″ divider, a 4″ compass with lengthening bar attachments, a bow compass, and bow dividers fulfills the average drafting requirements.

Bow instruments are better for small circles and measurements and for retaining a recurring dimension or arc. Their addition to a set gives greater drafting speed and flexibility.

The theatre requires very little drafting in ink. However, to be prepared for such rare occasions, a set can include a *ruling pen,* inking attachments for the compass, and a *bow* pen.

Most scenery is too large to be represented in a drawing at actual or full size, so it is necessary to reduce the size in regular proportions. The *scale rule* is devised to make the change in proportions as painless as possible. The most useful scale rule is the triangular form that provides twelve different graduations. It is

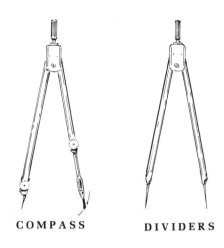

COMPASS   **DIVIDERS**

BOW COMPASS

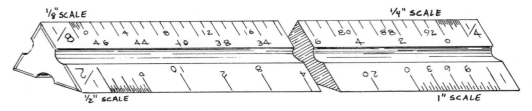

ARCHITECT'S SCALE
Triangular form, three faces, six edges, and twelve scales.

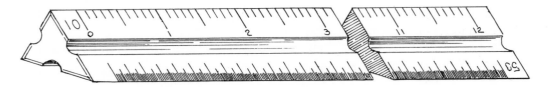

ENGINEER'S SCALE
Triangular form, three faces, six edges, and six scales.

nice to have many different graduations in one tool but sometimes time is lost in trying to find the correct scale. For this reason, many draftsmen like to use a set of scales that are individually graded to save time in finding the scale on the triangular form.

To the beginner, another confusing factor is the discovery that there are two types of scale rules: the architects' scale, which divides the proportional foot into twelfths or inches, and the engineers' scale, which divides the inch into decimals or tenths with divisions from ten to sixty. The names are trade names, not an indication of the profession using them. Engineers have as much use for the architects' scale as do architects. Inasmuch as stage settings, like houses, are built in feet and inches, the planning of scenery is done with the architects' scale rule.

Drawing pencils and *leads* for lead holders have varying degrees of hardness and softness. The soft lead produces a blacker line than the hard lead. The leads are graded by letters from 6B, which is very soft, through HB and H, which are medium soft to firm, to 6H, the hardest lead. A combination of H, 2H, and 4H leads gives the variety in line quality necessary for a good blueprint.

For clean-cut lines, a *sandpaper pad* or *flat file* keeps the proper point on the pencil or compass lead. There are mechanical-pencil pointers designed primarily for pointing leads of draftsmen's mechanical pencil or lead holder, but they will also point leads of wood pencils after the wood has been cut back with a knife.

Barring a genius from another world, the ownership of a pencil presupposes the need of an eraser. A *Ruby eraser* corrects pencil mistakes and an *Art Gum* eraser helps to keep the paper clean.

Drafting tape has more or less replaced thumbtacks for fastening paper to the drawing board. It is a quick easy method and it keeps the surface of the board free from tack holes that can snag a pencil and puncture a masterpiece.

The choice of paper depends, of course, on what type of drafting is planned. An ink drawing, a pencil drawing, or a preliminary study each requires different *tracing papers*. There are many kinds and no standardization of the numbering system, so the beginner is wise to seek the advice of a competent dealer. He can recommend the proper density of paper to ensure a clear, good contrast blueprint. Tracing paper in the roll is less expensive than by the pad. By choosing the width

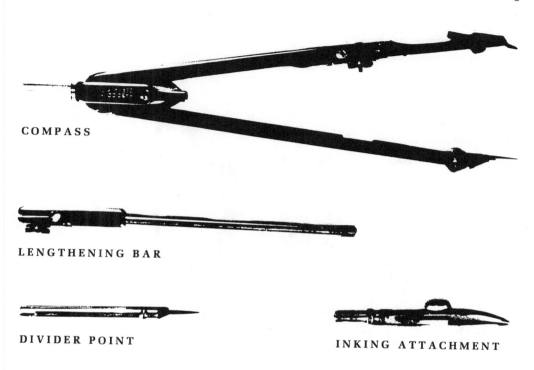

COMPASS

LENGTHENING BAR

DIVIDER POINT

INKING ATTACHMENT

SMALL DRAFTING SET

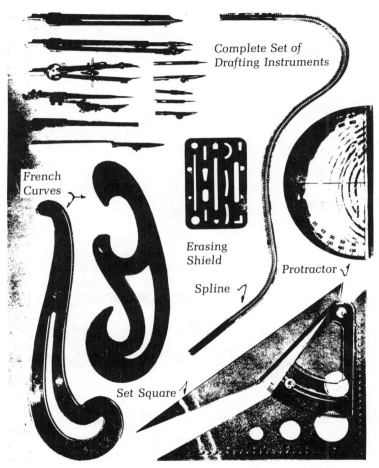

Complete Set of Drafting Instruments

French Curves

Erasing Shield

Spline

Protractor

Set Square

COMPLETE DRAFTING SET AND SOME HANDY ADDITIONAL TOOLS

of the roll, within one of the two dimensions of the drawing board, waste can be eliminated.

Drawing instruments and drafting tools represent a major investment but with proper care they can be handed down to the next generation. The life and usefulness of the T-square and triangles will be prolonged if they are put away flat or hung up. A T-square warps easily when it is left leaning in a corner. The head can be knocked out of square by using it as a hammer (this is a frequent misuse, believe it or not), or the edges of the blade can be ruined by using it as a knife guide.

The points on the dividers are very delicate and the arms can be easily sprung out of line or bent, if the dividers are used as a pick.

The scale rule isn't designed for use as a straightedge and, if it is used consistently for this purpose, the edge becomes so defaced the figures will be illegible.

And obviously, putting instruments away unclean, particularly the inking attachments, shortens their life and reduces their efficiency.

3

Viewpoint

In the theatre, drafting practices are so varied and loosely defined that it is difficult to catalog them. There are as many ways to draft a show as there are designers. If things are so disorganized, it may be asked, why bother to study any particular method? A close inspection reveals that each designer differs only in the amount of information given and in the way material is organized. All have in common a background of engineering drawing and its basic principle, the *orthographic projection*.

To the initiate, the term *orthographic projection* may seem remote. Relax! It is not as forbidding as it seems at first glance. *Ortho* means straight and *graphic* means line. In other words, a straight-line projection that is perpendicular to the surface in view. It may be simpler to understand if it is compared to the converging-line projection inherent in the foreshortening of a perspective drawing or photograph.

In a perspective drawing or photograph, a three-dimensional object is very descriptive and easy to visualize. Both represent perfectly a three-dimensional object in two dimensions. The object, however, is not represented in true proportion. As some surfaces are foreshortened, they are not seen in true dimension.

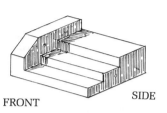

TOP

FRONT   SIDE

For example, it is easy to recognize the familiar three-step unit from a perspective drawing. The carpenter, however, needs more information than a pretty sketch. He wants to know its height, its width, and its depth. An orthographic projection is a draftsman's way of drawing the three-step to give this information.

The orthographic projection reveals an object, one view at a time, from all angles. The observer is free to move around the object to look at it from the top, from the front, from the sides, and if necessary, the viewer can look at the object from the bottom or rear. Each view is seen in true dimension by straight-line projection.

Obviously, a series of unrelated views of an object are of little value unless they

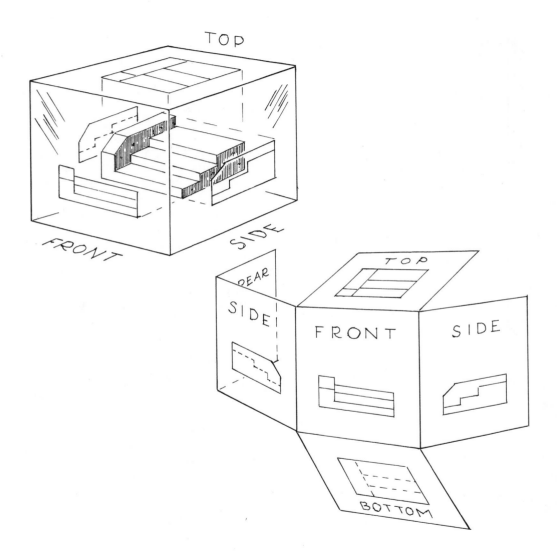

12

are organized in a connective manner to show the position of the object in space. Hence, there is a conventional arrangement of views that is the basis of all drafting techniques.

To understand the method of transposing the views of the object in space onto the drawing board requires some visual imagination. Using the three-step as an example, it is to be imagined in the center of a transparent cube. Projected on each side of the cube is a line drawing of the object as it appears in each view. With the side containing the front view as the center, the other faces of the cube are unfolded to either side, to the top, and to the bottom.

The front view is always the most recognizable view, showing the main characteristics of the object. It is the key view that gives the carpenter his bearings for visualizing the three-step unit in three dimensions. The top and side views are shown above and to the side of the front view and provide the three principal views of the object.

Borrowing from architecture, some views are referred to as *elevations*, a term that is applied to all views seen in a horizontal direction. The horizontal views include the front elevation, side elevations, and rear elevation.

An academic and less familiar expression is to refer to the views as *projections*. The front, top, and side views become respectively the vertical, horizontal, and profile projections. It is another way of describing the three principal planes of projection.

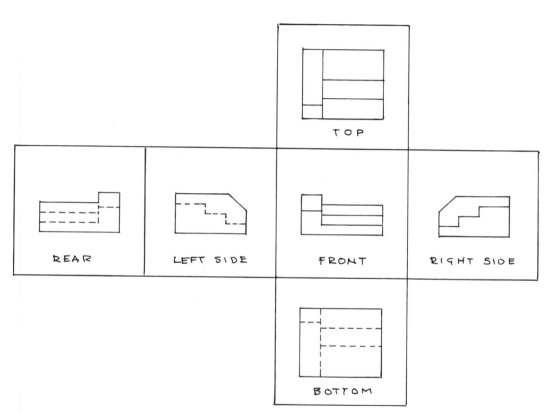

14

Another method of locating an object in space is to imagine the three principal planes of projection intersecting in space. The vertical plane intersects and passes through the horizontal plane at right angles. The profile plane passes through the vertical and horizontal planes and it is perpendicular to both of them. A view of the intersecting vertical and horizontal planes, looking toward the profile plane, reveals how the space is divided into quarters, or four quadrants. The quadrants are numbered counterclockwise, beginning with the upper right quadrant. Theoretically, an object can be placed in any of the quadrants and projected onto the three planes.

To transpose the projections onto the flat plane of the drawing board, the horizontal plane unfolds, downward, at the line of intersection with the vertical plane, while the profile plane unfolds to the right or left. With the planes unfolding in this manner, the projections in the second and fourth quadrants are superimposed on each other, and so they become confused and nearly useless. Only the first and third quadrants are practicable.

The regular orthographic projection described earlier is the same as a third-quadrant projection, for the planes unfold in this quadrant the same as the sides of the transparent cube. To standardize the relationship of views, the official American Standard used in all engineering drawing is classified as a third-quadrant projection.

When unfolded, a first-quadrant projection places the top view under the front view and reverses the direction of the side view. It is sometimes difficult to visualize the object from such an arrangement of views without being familiar with the first-quadrant projection. Architects use either the third or first quadrant, often

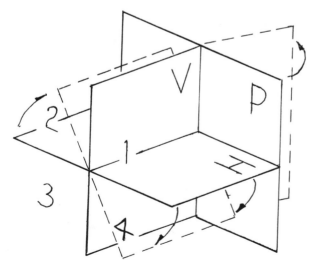

V: Vertical plane
H: Horizontal plane
P: Profile plane
1, 2, 3, 4: The four quadrants

placing the plan under the elevations. European designers' drawings and old drawings are frequently first-quadrant projections, and it is helpful to understand this system of projection although it may never be used as a method of drafting.

By this time it is apparent, that in either the first- or third-quadrant projection, the general relationship of views is the same. The order may be changed, or as often happens in the theatre, the views may be widely separated and sometimes drawn at different scale. Whatever the arrangement, the trained eye can visualize the object in space.

Of course, the carpenter doesn't refer to the drawings as third-quadrant projections or orthographic projections. To him they are working drawings. And that is precisely what they are, for with the simple addition of a few dimensions to the orthographic projection of the three-step, the carpenter is ready to start building.

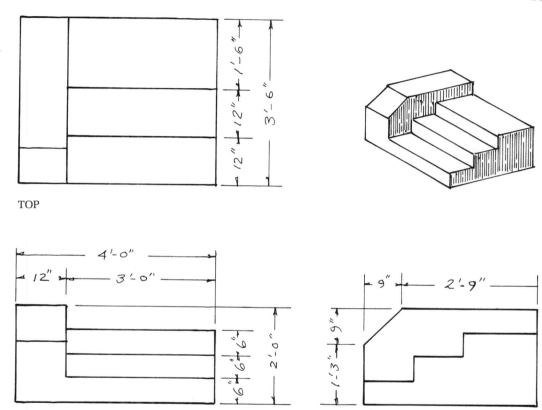

TOP

FRONT

SIDE

WORKING DRAWINGS

Designer's working drawings normally show three views drawn to scale and dimensioned. Occasionally, one view is omitted, or an additional view is included depending upon the complexity of the object.

4

Thick and Thin of It

The draftsman has a way of making the lines speak for themselves. In the draftsman's language, symbols and conventions are his words. His vocabulary has lines of all types. There are thick lines, thin lines, dotted lines, dashed lines, straight lines, and curved lines. Each has a different meaning and function. The draftsman's language, like any language, depends on a mutual knowledge of the symbols. The theatre, more than any other craft, relies on this mutual understanding to coordinate all phases of a stage production.

The first and simplest convention is the drawing of lines in different weights or thicknesses. The various types of line symbols are grouped into three weight classes: light, medium, and heavy. A line is made heavy or light depending on its eye-catching importance on the blueprint. Obviously, heavy lines are going to be seen first, medium-weight lines second, and lightweight lines last. Beyond the descriptive quality of the weight of a line there is the meaning or symbol of the function implied in the use of certain lines that needs to be explained.

It is easiest to begin with the medium-weight lines, for they are used the most and have already been seen in the working drawing of the three-step. They are the *outline lines* that represent the shape of the object, showing the edges and surfaces as they appear at the angle of the view. The visible outline is a solid line indicating the visible surfaces. The *hidden,* or *invisible, outline* is a dotted line indicating the hidden surfaces, not visible in the view.

Frequently the draftsman will want to show where an adjoining element of scenery touches the surface of an object or the alternate position of the same object. The *phantom line* symbolizes the removed object by outlining its position in the view. The designer has a choice of the symbols: a dashed line or the repetition of an elongated dash and two dots. Because a phantom line should always carry a label, the choice of line depends on the complexity of the outline of the removed part. Whichever symbol is chosen should be used consistently throughout the drawing.

The lightweight lines are many and varied in uses. Their function is to give additional information about the object and still not detract from the overall picture created by the outlines. That's why they are light in weight.

Dimension lines, with arrowheads at the ends, mark the extent of the surface that is being dimensioned. Figures, set into the line, show the exact distance. If dimension lines are set too close to the drawing or within the drawing, they may become confused with the outlines. To keep the dimension line away from the object, the *extension line* is used. They are solid and are drawn perpendicular to the surface of the object. As the name implies, they extend the surface to the dimension line. Although the arrowheads of the dimension line touch the extension line, the extension line itself is held clear of the object, about ¹⁄₁₆″ wherever possible.

Leaders, a relative of dimension lines, are made with one-sided arrowheads that touch the surface where a note or dimension applies. If the leader is always drawn slanted or curved, there is less chance for anyone to confuse it with the dimension line.

Break lines are space savers that denote a shortening of length or height. Occasionally, the draftsman wants to draw a unit of scenery too long to fit on the paper. He can reduce the length by taking a piece out of the center and using a break line to show that the piece is not represented in full length. The break line can also be used to indicate that the outer surface of an object has been cut away to show inner structure. The *long break line* is a straight line with spasmodic eruptions occurring at intervals, while the *short break line* is a more subtle curve with less regularity.

A *hidden construction line* is a repeated dot or small dash indicating rear construction such as bracing, picture battens, or covered hinging.

Finally, there is the *center line* symbolized by an alternate dash and dot. The center line is used to establish the center of the circles and the dividing line of symmetrical parts. It is a familiar symbol in the floor plan of a stage setting where it marks the center of the proscenium opening. The center line is an important reference line for the location of a set on the stage.

Heavyweight lines are used solely to indicate the cross section of an object. A section is the cutting away and removing of a portion of an object to reveal the inside.

LIGHTWEIGHT LINES

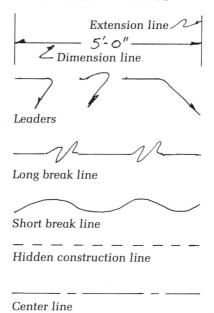

Extension line

5'-0"

Dimension line

Leaders

Long break line

Short break line

Hidden construction line

Center line

MEDIUM-WEIGHT LINES

Visible outline

Hidden outline

Phantom lines

Cutting plane lines, drawn over an adjoining view, are a repeating dash and double dot. The arrowheads point the direction seen in the sectional view.

Section outlines are heavy solid lines around the cut surfaces in the sectional view. They emphasize the cut surface over the uncut surface. Cut surfaces are further set apart by the use of *section lines,* a lightweight crosshatching within the section outline. The sections are varied

in pattern and direction to indicate a change in material, or a different structural member.

Drafting in Pencil and Ink

When drafting in pencil, the varying weights of lines are determined by the hardness or softness of the lead that is used. As it has been suggested, on a normally hard surface the 4H lead produces a lightweight line, the 2H lead is good for the medium-weight outline, and the H lead is excellent for the heavyweight line. This will vary up or down a degree depending on the hardness of the drafting surface. A soft surface, for example, requires softer pencils to get the same weight of line. With a little experimentation, the beginner can find the set of pencils or leads that are best suited for his use. The choice is arbitrary and varies with each draftsman. Some skilled draftsmen are able to obtain a full range of line quality with only one pencil for the entire drawing.

Although most scene designers draft in pencil, some technical drawings are done in ink. The Rapidograph, technical fountain pen, is excellent for this purpose. It has a long point for working against a

straightedge and provides a nonclogging flow of ink. The pen uses India ink, which is opaque for clear reproduction, dries quickly, and does not smear from erasing. The most useful points for normal drafting are sizes 0 and 1.

HEAVYWEIGHT LINES

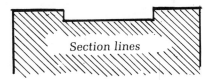

Cutting plane line

Section outline

Section lines

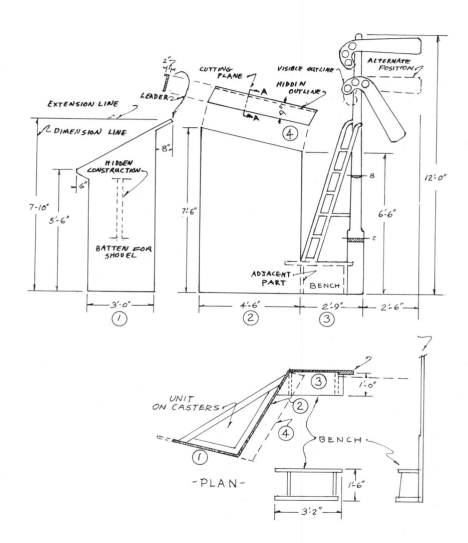

Designer's drawings of a small set piece showing the use of the various types of lines.

5

Inside Story

Everyone has seen a curious youngster taking a new toy apart to see what is inside. Conversely, the designer many times finds it easier to explain a three-dimensional piece of scenery by cutting it open and showing the inner structure. The *section* is the draftsman's way of performing the same operation. A revealing show-all-hide-nothing view is a great time and space saver, and in the theatre, it can be used in many different ways.

The sectional view is made by cutting into the object with a *cutting plane,* an imaginary plane that cuts like a giant knife and divides the object into halves. With imagination one half of the object is removed exposing the inside of the other half. The *cutting plane line* shows the location of the cut and the arrowheads indicate the direction of the view. The location of the cutting plane is arbitrary, and if it is placed wisely, the sectional view will tell all. The cutting plane can be staggered or offset, forward and back to include a special detail. In the offset section, however, it is important to show the offset of the cutting plane line clearly so the viewer can read the section correctly.

Usually, the cutting plane is vertical and most sectional views are vertical sections. There are occasions, however, when a horizontal section is necessary. The cut-

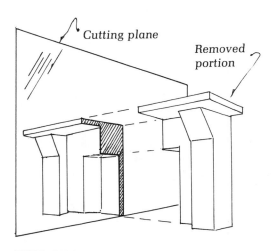

THE SECTION

ting plane is used in a horizontal position and the resulting section is referred to as a plan.

The floor plan of a stage set is a horizontal section with a cutting plane that is parallel to the stage floor. To expose the true shape and structure of the set, the cutting plane is passed through as many wall openings as possible. The upper portion is removed and the direction of the view is downward. There are times when the lower portion is removed to show a view looking upward, possibly at an elaborate ceiling or cornice design.

A plan differs from a regular section in one respect. When the drawing is labeled as a plan, it is not necessary to show a cutting plane line on the adjoining elevation, or front view, because it is understood that the cutting plane is horizontal.

There are many ways to show the inside of an object and sometimes it isn't necessary to use a separate sectional view. One short cut is the *half section*. If the object is symmetrical and it is felt a section is needed to explain the internal design, space can be saved by using a half section. Only half of the outer surface is removed so the cutting plane turns at right angles on the center line and cuts out a portion like a piece of pie. The half-section view stops at the center line and shares the rest of the space with the elevation, or front view.

A similar effect can be obtained with a *broken-out section*. It, too, is a partial section but the outer surface is broken or peeled away, like peeling an orange, rather than a clean cut on the center line. The broken-out portion is drawn right on the exterior view, showing as much of the interior as is thought necessary. The use of this type of sectional view in the theatre is rather limited. The floor plan of a double-decked or two-level set might require a broken-out section to explain the

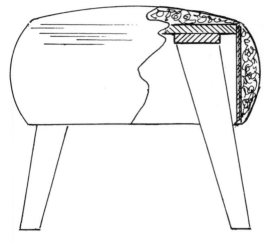

A BROKEN-OUT SECTION

change in level. Sometimes it is used to explain a complicated piece of scenery more as an illustration than as a working drawing.

Other uses of the section are the *revolved section* and the *removed section*, two convenient ways of showing the shape of an object without using a full section view. The revolved section is drawn right on the exterior view by passing the cutting plane perpendicular to the axis of the part to be sectioned, then the plane is revolved into view. At small scale, the revolved section does little more than in-

dicate a change of shape. If the silhouette of the section is important to the design, a larger or full-scale view should be included.

The removed section is used to explain the irregular shapes that occur so frequently in the theatre. Rock pieces, tree trunks, and abstract forms have to be designed and drafted the same as the more standard shapes. A removed section is made the same way as a revolved section, but instead of drawing it within the view, it is removed or set outside the view. When the shape is not uniform, several sections may be used to show the changing contour. In such cases, each section is carefully related to its cutting plane with reference letters.

All the sectional views are extremely useful to the designer, for they often give more descriptive information than the normal front, top, and side views. With the use of a section he can frequently eliminate one or more of the conventional views that not only save time and space drafting but also make the blueprint easier to read and understand.

Like the youngster and disassembled toy, the carpenter is asking similar questions of a new set of working drawings. Where does this piece go? What holds it up? How does it all fit together? The *as-*

sembled drawing is used to answer these questions, especially if the set has unusual shapes or complicated movement and construction.

The assembled drawing can be made from any angle or view that best shows the relative position of the different parts. It can be a full exterior view showing the assembled pieces in position. It can be an exterior view with a portion of the inside revealed by means of the broken-out section or half section. It can be a full section showing the assembled parts in a cross-sectional view. In all cases, if each part of the assembled drawing is numbered to correspond with the labeling of the separate view of the part, it is easy to show how a set, or portion of a set, fits together.

The floor plan of a stage setting is an assembled drawing, for it shows the relationship of each piece of scenery. The average set is readily explained with the use of a clearly labeled floor plan and a set of elevations of the walls.

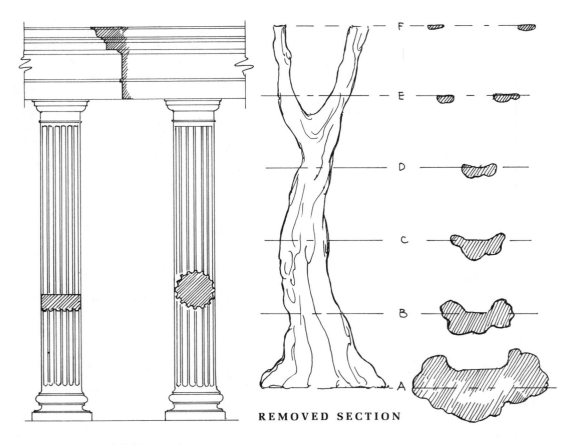

REVOLVED SECTIONS

REMOVED SECTION

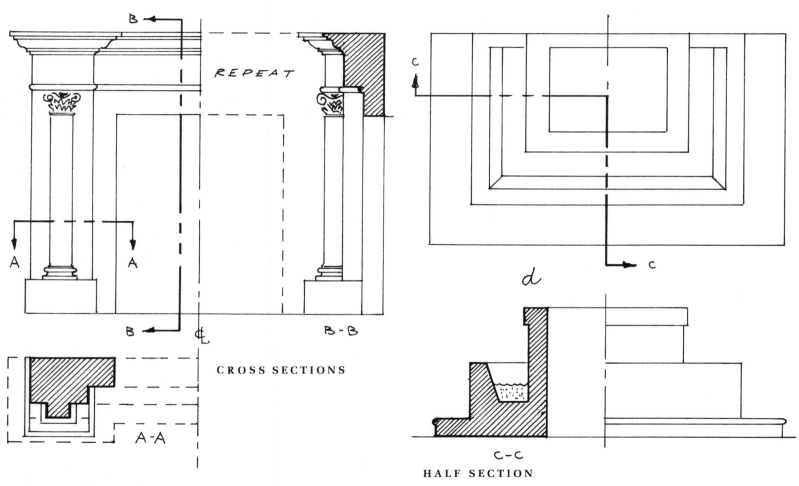

vertical

B

REPEAT

c

A   A

d

B   ℄

B – B

c

CROSS SECTIONS

A – A

horizontal

C – C

HALF SECTION

6

Feet and Inches

To the many questions the carpenter asks about a new set of working drawings, might be added, how big is it? Although he may understand the drawings, he can't begin to build until he has some indication of size. A carpenter relies on a scaled drawing, or a dimensioned drawing, for such information.

Most of the misunderstandings that occur between the drawing board and the finished set are over dimensions, such as the wall that is too small for the sofa or doors that are too large for the openings. The carpenter is often fit to chew nails, with an unscaled drawing, vital dimensions missing, when he discovers the designer is off to remote parts in search of a nineteenth-century crocheted tea cosy.

The dimensions that are put on the drawing are not only the ones that were used to develop the drawing but those that will help the carpenter lay out and construct the piece in the shop. To think through the construction doesn't usurp the carpenter's place in the theatre. It is, however, a constant reminder of the importance of dimensions.

As it has been pointed out, the dimension line is a lightweight line with arrowheads at either end to indicate the extent of the surface being dimensioned. The figures, running parallel to the dimension line, are set above the line or into the line. The latter method, though taking more time to draw, leaves less room for confusion.

The scale of most scenery makes it impractical to dimension in inches unless the distance is under a foot. The figures are in inches up to 12″ then in feet and inches, such as 1′6″. There is too much of a chance that small dimensions over a foot, such as 18″, might be mistaken for 1′8″.

When the dimension line is perpendicular, the figures read upward. On a slanted dimension line right of perpendicular, the figures read upward and conversely; they read downward on a slanted dimension line left of perpendicular. In other words, all dimensions are read from the bottom or right-hand side of the blueprint.

Automotive and aircraft industries have the practice of setting the figures into the dimension line horizontally regardless of the direction of the line. All figures can be read from the bottom of the print. Although such practice saves time in drafting, it occupies considerably more space. Either method is adaptable to drafting in the theatre as long as one is consistent throughout the drawing.

The position of a dimension can cause confusion. The placement, of course, depends on the shape and structure of the object. As a general rule, if the dimensions are kept outside the view and between views as much as possible, the chances of confusing them with the object's outline are reduced.

Another opportunity for confusion is to combine line symbols. For example, a dimension can be carried *to* a center line, but it is not wise to use the center line *as* a dimension line. The center line is a symbol with a specific function, and if used as a dimension line, it can easily lose its identity.

It isn't necessary to repeat dimensions unless the views are widely separated or on different sheets. The dimensions should be complete. It doesn't pay to be lazy and require the carpenter to add or subtract unless his arithmetic is considered superior.

The placement of dimensions can become quite involved when a piece of scenery has intricate edges and complex surfaces. It is good practice to think about placement of dimensions before arranging the drawings on the paper. If it looks complicated, plenty of space should be allowed between views, or the scale enlarged. The cost of an extra sheet of paper is small compared to a mistake caused by confusing an overcrowded dimension.

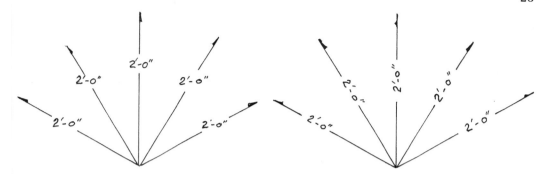

SETTING DIMENSIONS

Two methods of setting dimensions into dimension line. Left, reads from bottom of page. Right, reads from bottom and right side. Both are acceptable but should be used consistently throughout drawing.

The clearest and easiest placement of a group of dimensions is in a *continuous line*. If the shape of the object does not permit the use of continuous dimension in a straight line, it can be staggered to follow the contours of the edge.

If the surfaces are in a regular or symmetrical pattern, the dimensions can be given in parallel lines. Parallel dimensions are easier to read than continuous line, but they give less useable information to the carpenter.

Similar to the parallel dimension, and more frequently used in the theatre, is the base-line dimension. Rather than in a continuous line, all dimensions are given from a base or reference line. An example of a base line is the floor, or bottom edge of a wing. Many dimensions are given in terms of height, or distance off the floor. The center line and set line of the floor plan are base lines that are perpendicular to each other. The floor plan is dimensioned from these two reference lines.

The carpenter uses the base-line technique to layout or locate an opening in a wing, but he also wants to know distances between points. The best use of base-line dimensions in the theatre is to point out, or emphasize, important heights and distances along with the more inclusive continuous-line dimension. It serves as a check for the cumulative errors that can occur by measuring from point to point. The carpenter also likes to see overall dimensions so he can quickly calculate the size of a piece of scenery without a lot of addition or subtraction. The overall dimension also serves as a double check of the total of the smaller dimensions.

At the scale most scenery is drafted, the smaller surfaces are sometimes so small that the dimension line and figures can't be set into the space between the extensions lines. A *limited space dimension* is set to one side and a leader is used to indicate where it applies.

Circles and *arcs* are dimensioned in a special way. To construct a circle or arc in the shop, the carpenter wants to know two things—What is the radius? Where is the center? If a circle is large enough, it can be dimensioned on a radius line drawn within the circumference. The radius becomes a dimension line with the figures and an uppercase R, for radius, set into the line. Beginning at the center, the line is drawn at an angle to avoid confusion with the center lines, and it ends with an arrowhead touching the circumference. The center, of course, is located with a pair of dimension lines. A portion of a circle or arc can be dimensioned in the same manner.

There are two ways to dimension an angle. One is to state the number of de-

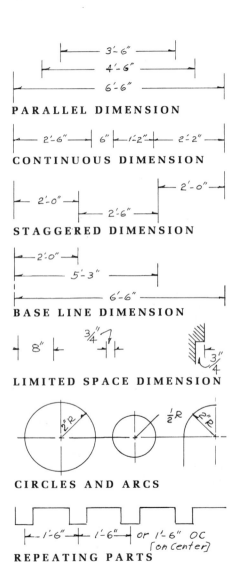

PARALLEL DIMENSION

CONTINUOUS DIMENSION

STAGGERED DIMENSION

BASE LINE DIMENSION

LIMITED SPACE DIMENSION

CIRCLES AND ARCS

REPEATING PARTS

grees between the two intersecting lines, or a line and the floor. The other is to give the angle in terms of perpendicular dimensions. For example, a slanted surface may be shown to have a rise of 2′ over a distance of 4′. The carpenter needs to know these two dimensions even if it is stated that the angle of the incline is approximately 27°. At small scale it is difficult to use a protractor accurately. Unless the angle is standard, or the scale of the drafting very large, it is safer to use the two perpendicular dimensions.

For an edge with a recurring shape or an object made up of duplicate parts, it isn't necessary to use a continuous dimension unless the spacing varies. It is easier to assemble repeating parts in the shop if the space from center to center is given. Once the size of the part is established, the spacing can be noted as so many feet or inches OC—on center.

Irregular edges of a cutout, or set piece, are often too complicated to dimension other than indicating the overall size. The edge can be reproduced with a high degree of accuracy if it is overlaid with a grid of 1′ squares. The squares are in the scale of the drawing and they may be larger or smaller depending on the intricacy of the design. For the important design details that must be duplicated with complete accuracy, it is wise to give the

METHODS OF INDICATING SLOPE

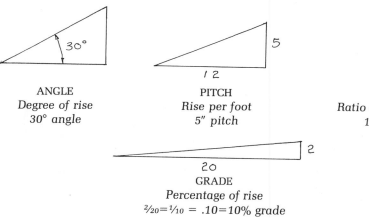

ANGLE
Degree of rise
30° angle

PITCH
Rise per foot
5" pitch

BATTER
Ratio of rise to base
1:4 batter

GRADE
Percentage of rise
$^2/_{20} = {}^1/_{10} = .10 = 10\%$ grade

carpenter a set of full-scale drawings or patterns.

An essential part of accurate dimensioning is the ability to work at a fixed proportion. Except for a few details, most scenery is drafted at a reduced scale of one-half inch to a foot in actual size. It is referred to as ½" scale, or simply ½ scale. The new draftsman will want to become familiar with his scale rule to learn how to read and measure with it.

A close examination of the triangular scale rule will reveal that the edge of each face is marked with two scales. Each scale is designated with a number or fraction and is read towards the opposite end. For example, if the scale is turned to the edge marked 1 at the left, the opposite, or right end is marked ½. The figure 1 on the left is the scale of 1" = 1'0". Beginning at the zero and moving to the right are the one-foot markings. Left of the zero is a one-foot space divided into twelfths. These are the inch markings at one-inch scale.

The same thing is true of the ½" scale at the opposite end, except that the inch markings are right of the zero, while the foot markings are left of the zero and in even numbers. All the scales, as a turn of the rule will show, are treated in the same manner.

A change in proportion can also be referred to as a change in size. An object

TWO METHODS OF DIMENSIONING
IRREGULAR SHAPES

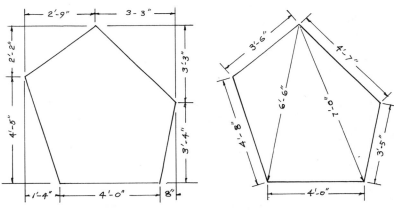

A. Using perpendicular dimensions   B. Using triangulation (page 83)

DIMENSIONED SET PIECE USING AN OVERLAID GRID

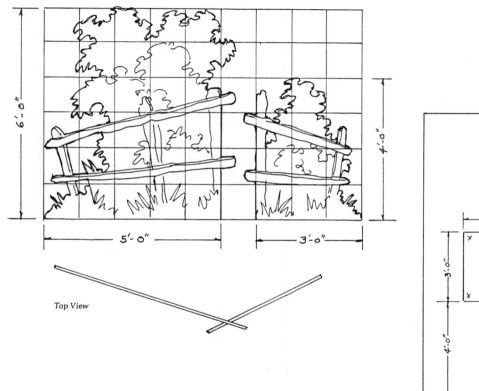

Top View

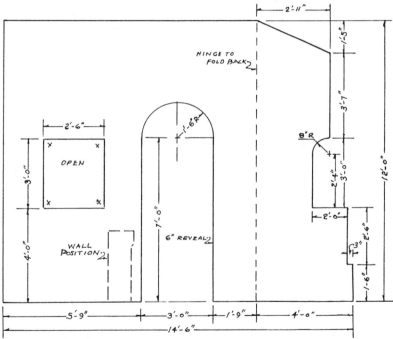

ELEVATION DIMENSIONS

A sample of the designer's front elevation or working drawings illustrating many types of dimensions.

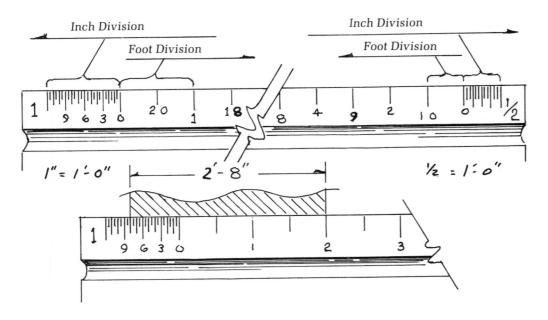

Inch Division   Inch Division
Foot Division   Foot Division

1" = 1'-0" |—— 2'-8" ——| ½ = 1'-0"

SAMPLE READING AT 1" SCALE

may be drawn at half-size. It is not the same as ½ scale, because an object drawn at half-size is at the scale of 6" = 1'0", or ½' = 1'0". Quarter-size is the largest size shown on the normal architects' scale. The scale 3" = 1'0" is quarter-size.

The Metric Scale Rule

There are firm indications that in the near future the United States will join the majority of nations and convert to the metric system of measurement. Leading up to that event and briefly after the changeover there will be a period of constant cross-reference until feet and inches have been wiped out of the mind as a scale refer-

ence. Meanwhile, the theatre draftsman may be required to know and use both systems. Present-day theatre already experiences plans and construction drawings for European and British imports that are usually in meters and have to be transposed into feet and inches or executed in meters.

The metric drafting-scale rule illustrated is a fully divided rule and uses two basic divisions: the millimeter (mm) and the meter (m), which is 1,000 mm. The ratio of the scale is 1:5 and 1:50 respectively. Although not indicated on the rule, the centimeter (cm) can be determined by noting every 100 mm or by moving the decimal point of the reading.

To transpose or integrate the two systems, the basic point of reference is that 25 mm is approximately equal to 1", which is an easy number to remember if it is necessary to convert or refer to feet and inches. Hence the ratios 1:12.5 is approximately 1" scale, 1:25 m = ½" scale, 1:50 m = ¼" scale, and so on.

There is a conversion scale rule from Britain designed to convert metric ratio to imperial dimensions. It is an open divided-scale similar to the architects' scale. The illustration shows the ratio 1:24 as being equal to ½" scale (½" = 1'0"). This odd ratio is formulated by the

METRIC SCALE RULES AND TAPES

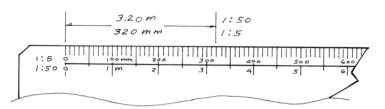

FULLY DIVIDED METRIC DRAFTING SCALE RULE

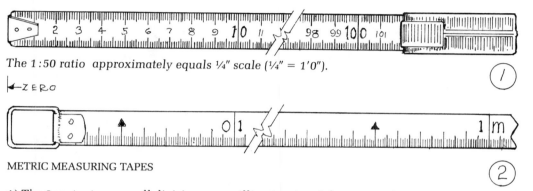

The 1:50 ratio approximately equals ¼" scale (¼" = 1'0").

METRIC MEASURING TAPES

1) The 3-meter tape: small divisions are millimeters (mm), larger, centimeters (cm). 2) 30-meter tape: major divisions are at 10 centimeters (.01 meters).

division of the imperial inch into twenty-fourths. Hence 1:12 equals 1" scale, 1:24 equals ½" scale, 1:48 equals ¼" scale, and so on.

When drafting at a reduced scale, it is important to remember that either of the conversion methods are approximations and can develop errors over longer dimensions. If we assume, for example, 25 mm per inch, it totals to a 40" meter, which conversion tables show more accurately to be 39.37 inches.

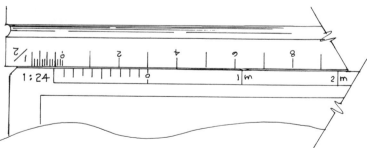

METRIC-CONVERSION SCALE RULE

Open divided-scale showing the metric ratio 1:24 as being equal to ½" scale (½" = 1'0").

7

Another Angle

Many solid or three-dimensional pieces of scenery are regular architectural forms, such as steps, columns, newel posts, and the like, and they are very easily explained in the orthographic technique. The usual front, side, and top views give the carpenter all the information he needs. However, some pieces have slanted sides or are angled, either to increase the perspective or to distort them for design purposes. Whatever the reason, there is the problem of drawing a surface that is inclined to two, or more, of the principal planes of projection. The regular front, side, and top views do not show the inclined surface in true dimension.

Carrying the orthographic technique a step further, the observer is free to move around the object to the angle that allows a view straight at the slanted surface. From this perpendicular view, the surface is seen in true shape. Because it is not one of the normal views, it is known as an *auxiliary view*. The process of getting an auxiliary view onto the drawing board requires the use of a new plane of projection, a reference plane, and a generous amount of visual imagination.

At a position opposite the auxiliary face, there is imagined a plane that is parallel to the slant of the face and containing a projection of the surface in true shape. The plane is not one of the principal planes of projection, so it is referred to as an *auxiliary plane*. It is usually perpendicular to one of the principal planes of projection and it is slanted to the other two. This means that in one of the three views, the slanted surface is seen from the edge, or in profile, and it appears as a line. The auxiliary plane, being parallel to the auxiliary face, also appears as a line and is rotated onto the plane of the paper to reveal the projection of the true shape.

The hinge of the rotation is the intersection of the auxiliary plane and the *reference plane* (a second imaginary plane that is always located perpendicular to the auxiliary plane and, consequently, is usually parallel to one of the principal planes of projection). The reference plane, like the base line, is used to establish distances and the location of points on the slanted surface. The reference plane always appears as a line because it is only seen in edge view, or as it intersects the auxiliary plane. The auxiliary plane, of course, is only shown in its rotated position revealing the projection of the auxiliary face.

Because the edge view of the slanted surface may occur in any one of the principal views, an auxiliary view may be

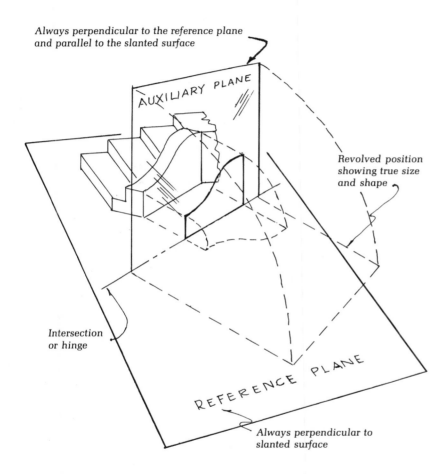

Always perpendicular to the reference plane and parallel to the slanted surface

AUXILIARY PLANE

Revolved position showing true size and shape

Intersection or hinge

REFERENCE PLANE

Always perpendicular to slanted surface

AUXILIARY ELEVATION
The slanted surface is perpendicular to the horizontal plane and angled to the vertical and profile planes.

drawn opposite a front view, a side view, or a top view, depending on the direction of the incline. In an *auxiliary elevation*, for example, the slanted surface is perpendicular to the horizontal plane and it is angled to the vertical and profile planes. The edge of the slanted surface is seen in the top view.

The auxiliary elevation is started opposite the edge view of the slanted surface in the top view by drawing, at a convenient distance, a parallel line to establish the intersection of the reference plane and the auxiliary plane. It is represented with a repeating dash and double-dot symbol, the same as the cutting plane line. In many respects, the reference plane is similar to the cutting plane of a section except that it isn't always passed through the object. The reference plane is sometimes passed to one side, and in the case of the auxiliary elevation, it is located underneath the object.

To develop the auxiliary view, all heights are measured from the horizontal reference plane and all horizontal dimensions are projected from the top view. The distances off the floor that appear in the front or side elevation are transferred to the auxiliary view as perpendicular distances from the reference plane. It is customary to show, in the completed drawing, only the slanted surface because the auxiliary view tends to foreshorten the rest of the object.

If the angled surface is slanted to one side or the other it is referred to as a *right* or *left* auxiliary view. Here the auxiliary plane is perpendicular to the vertical plane. It is slanted to the horizontal and profile plane. The reference plane is a vertical or frontal plane and the edge view of the slanted surface is in the front view. The auxiliary view is located opposite the slanted surface in the front view. If the slanted surface is symmetrical, the reference plane line can be a center line in the top view. Then the auxiliary view pivots like a revolving door about the bisecting reference line.

A surface ramped forward or back has a *front* or *rear* auxiliary view. The auxiliary plane is perpendicular to the profile plane and it is angled to the vertical and horizontal planes. The edge view is in the side view and opposite it is drawn the auxiliary view. The reference plane is parallel to the profile plane.

By now the question may be raised, What about the surface that is angled to all three of the principal planes of projection?

An oblique surface of such a nature frequently occurs in a stage set and, to show it, involves the use of an *oblique* auxiliary view. Because the surface is askew to

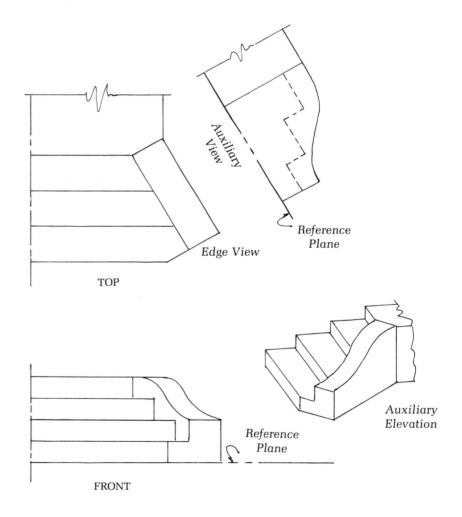

TOP

Auxiliary View

Edge View

Reference Plane

FRONT

Reference Plane

Auxiliary Elevation

AUXILIARY ELEVATION

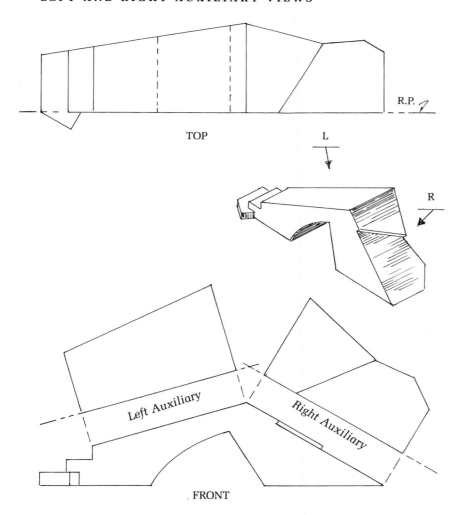

LEFT AND RIGHT AUXILIARY VIEWS

R.P.

TOP

L

R

Left Auxiliary

Right Auxiliary

FRONT

36

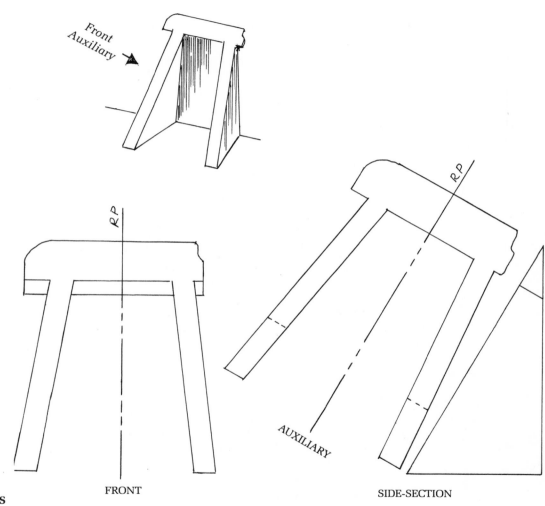

Front
Auxiliary

RP

RP

FRONT

AUXILIARY

SIDE-SECTION

FRONT AND REAR AUXILIARY VIEWS

OBLIQUE AUXILIARY VIEW

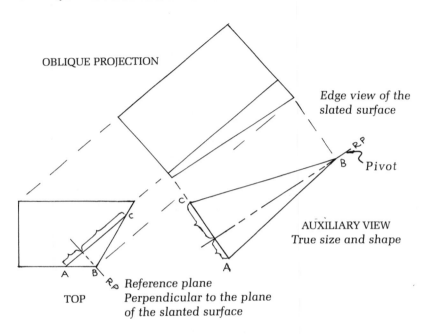

OBLIQUE PROJECTION

Edge view of the slated surface

B · *Pivot*

AUXILIARY VIEW
True size and shape

TOP

Reference plane
Perpendicular to the plane
of the slanted surface

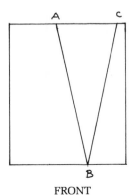

A   C

B

FRONT

Plane ABC is askew to all three principal planes of projection. Line AC of plane ABC is parallel to the ground. The oblique projection is an elevational view showing the surface ABC in edge view. The auxiliary view is developed, opposite the edge view and perpendicular to the reference plane, in the usual manner.

all principal planes of projection, the edge view is not shown in any of the regular views. It becomes necessary first to draw an *oblique projection* of the object that will show an edge view of the angled surface. The angle of the projection is established on a line parallel to one of the sides of the slanted surface. In the other types of auxiliary views the reference plane, as well as being parallel to a principal plane, has always been perpendicular to the plane of the slanted surface. This is accomplished by passing a plane in the view opposite the oblique projection and perpendicular to the oblique lines of projection. The hinge, or reference line, is constructed parallel to the edge view in the oblique projection. The auxiliary plane is unfolded into view in the usual manner.

All auxiliary views, in general, work best with smaller pieces of angled scenery, steps, and platforms where the scale can be increased and give the view enough accuracy to be used as a working drawing. For large pieces of scenery with oblique angles, the auxiliary view is awkward and at the necessarily small scale, it is inaccurate. Inasmuch as the larger pieces probably will not be in three dimensions but will knock down into a series of flat planes, it is easier to find true size and shape by other methods.

8

Pictorials

A draftsman many times has the need for pictorial drawings, either to help clarify the form of an object in his own mind or to help someone with an untrained imagination visualize the object from the orthographic views. In a sense, the designer's perspective sketch performs this function. The sketch is of limited use to the carpenter, obviously, because of the foreshortening in the perspective.

By imagining a pictorial drawing with the edges of the receding surfaces *not* converging and sides *not* foreshortened, a type of pictorial is represented that can be drawn to scale and used as a supplementary view to the working drawings. The lack of perspective makes it possible to draw to scale. As a view, however, it has a distorted mechanical look and it is limited in its representation of curves and angles. The best use is as a pictorial view of a structural, or mechanical, detail that is not clear in the regular orthographic views.

The beginning of a pictorial drawing depends on the angle, or viewpoint, desired of the object. If it is to be, for example, a pictorial of a cube, it must be decided first how it is to look. Is it to be drawn as seen from a corner? Or is it to be viewed from one side? Is it to be seen from above looking down or from underneath looking up? The shape of the object and the location of details affect the choice of the direction of the view.

With an object as simple as a cube, a view from a corner and slightly above represents it with the least amount of distortion. Such is the usual direction of an *isometric* drawing, for it is started with an edge of the cube touching the plane of the paper, or *picture plane*, as it is called.

The term *isometric*, meaning equal measure as compared to the foreshortened distances, or unequal-measure of perspective, accurately describes its appearance. An isometric drawing has three axes to represent the principal planes. The first is a vertical line to indicate all the upright edges; second, a slanted line to the right, 30° to the horizontal, for the horizontal edges of the right plane; and third, a 30° line slanted to the left to represent the horizontal edges of planes to the left. These lines and all lines parallel to them are known as *isometric lines*. Conversely, lines that are not parallel to any of the three axes are *nonisometric* lines. Heights and distances can be measured on isometric lines but a nonisometric line cannot be drawn to scale.

Returning to the cube, if it is 2′ in height and width and is to be drawn at a scale of 1″ = 1′0″, the isometric drawing can be started by measuring off a 2″ vertical axis for the nearest upright edge. An isometric drawing can be started from the top surface and measured down, or from the bottom edges, and develop the shape upward. The shape of the object sometimes determines how it is to be developed. As most scenery sits on the floor or on a level surface, it is easiest to develop the isometric from the floor upward.

The two remaining isometric axes are attached to the lower end of the vertical axis, extended in opposite directions and slanted upward at 30°. At a point 2″ from the vertical axis on each slanted isometric line, a pair of vertical lines are drawn representing two more vertical edges of the cube.

The top edges of the two nearest faces of the cube are drawn with lines that are parallel to the base and at a height of 2″. The top is completed by drawing the top edges of the two rear faces of the cube. These edges are made by two slanted lines converging from the opposite corners. Unless the drafting is inaccurate, they will measure 2″ in length.

Hidden lines are omitted in an isometric unless they are needed to further describe the object. If the diagonals of one of the sides or of the top of the isometric cube are drawn and measured,

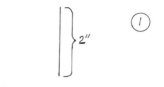
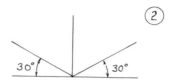
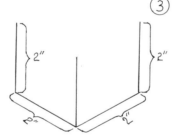

1. Vertical axis
2. Horizontal axis
3. Vertical edges of cube
4. Completed isometric of cube

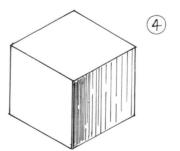
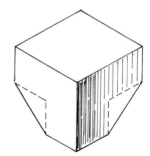

Use of hidden lines

they prove to be unequal in length. They are nonisometric lines, and therefore, they are not seen in true dimension. A nonisometric line is drawn by locating points with isometric lines that are on, or at the ends of, the angled line and then connect the points to form the line. An irregular curve is plotted in the same manner. Enough points on the curve are located with isometric lines so that the curve can be redrawn in isometric.

An irregular shape is difficult to draw in isometric and usually it looks so misshapen that there is little value in the pictorial view unless it explains a mechanical detail or tricky assembly.

A regular curve or circle can be plotted and drawn freehand, the same as an irregular curve. There is a method, however, of approximating a circle or arc in isometric with a compass. 1) The circle is enclosed in a square. 2) The square is located on the object and drawn in isometric. The next step is to draw the circle within the isometric square, tangent to each side at midpoint as it was in the regular view. The sides of the isometric square are isometric lines, so they can be measured to find the midpoint. 3) At midpoint, a line is drawn perpendicular to the side and extending into the square. When all four perpendicular bisectors are

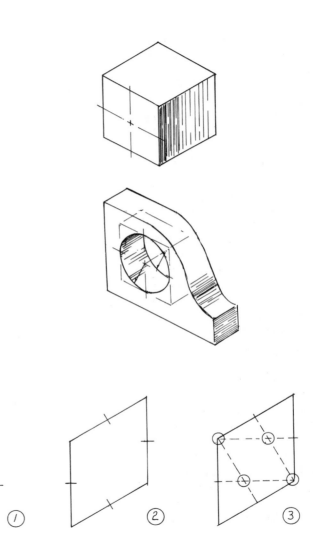

drawn there are four points of intersection. 4) Starting opposite the small, or acute, angle and using the intersection of the perpendicular bisectors of the adjoining sides as a center, an arc is swung that is tangent to both sides. 5) In front of the obtuse angle, the radius of the arc will be longer, for the perpendicular bisectors are spread by the wider angle and intersect at a greater distance from the sides. 6) The remaining arcs are drawn by the same method to complete the isometric circle. It can be easily seen that to speed up the drafting of the approximation of a circle

both small arcs can be drawn before changing the compass setting for the larger arcs.

A circle can be drawn into any of the principal planes of the isometric by the same method, but if the circle is on a nonisometric plane, it cannot be approximated and so it has to be drawn by the point plotting method.

Depth, or thickness, of an arch can be drawn by moving the center of the arcs forward or backward, the distance of the thickness along a line parallel to an isometric line.

To vary the direction of the view and

look at the object from underneath, the axes are reversed. The axis of the horizontal edge is now angled down 30° and to the right and left. It is also possible to turn the main vertical axis into a horizontal position to show a long narrow object.

Because of the nature of pictorials an isometric drawing may be dimensioned like a working drawing. The technique, however, is slightly different. Instead of being perpendicular to the surface, the extension lines are drawn as extensions of one of the isometric planes, and the dimension line is parallel to the edge of the

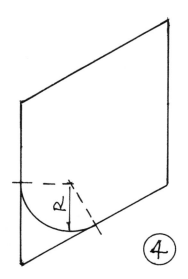

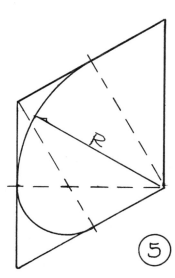

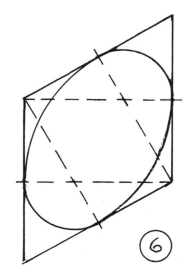

42

object rather than perpendicular to the extension line. To help give the feeling that the dimension is in one of the isometric planes, the figures are slanted with the extension lines. If the object is not too complicated, a dimensioned pictorial drawing can be used as a working drawing.

It is apparent by now how irregular edges, curves, and angles are distorted in the isometric view, and it may be desirable to change the direction of the view to show them at a better advantage. By moving around the object until the complicated surface is parallel to the picture plane, it is possible to see the irregular edge or curve without distortion. A feeling of third dimension is accomplished by drawing the side and top of the object at an oblique angle to the right or left.

A pictorial view from this direction is an *oblique* drawing. The same general pictorial characteristics are present in the oblique drawing as in the isometric with the exception of a more pronounced distortion in the appearance. Because of the frontal position of one of the principal planes, two of the oblique axes are at right angles to each other. The angle of the third axis, representing the plane of the sides, may vary from 30° to 45° to the horizontal. It can be drawn to the right or

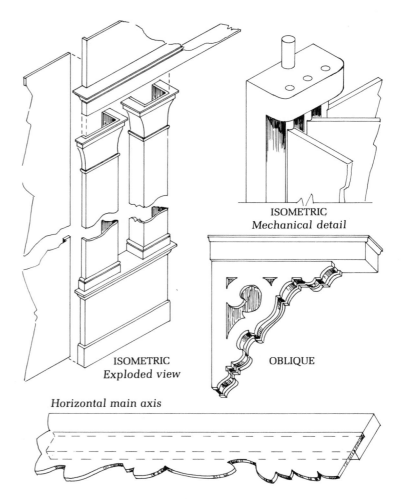

ISOMETRIC
Mechanical detail

ISOMETRIC
Exploded view

OBLIQUE

Horizontal main axis

PICTORIAL DRAWINGS

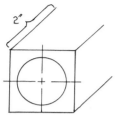

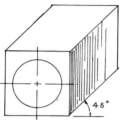

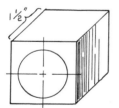

OBLIQUE DRAWING

CABINET 3–4

left and slanted up or down. The oblique drawing is more flexible than the isometric because of the greater variety of views.

Although the construction of the oblique drawing in relation to its axes is the same as the isometric, there is a difference in the way the drawing is started. The oblique drawing begins with the frontal plane rather than an edge, as in the isometric. The parallel position of this surface makes the first step essentially a front view of the object. Therefore, the side of the object that is chosen to be placed parallel to the picture plane is the most complicated surface. By placing the side that contains the irregular outlines, angles, and curves in the frontal position, drafting time can be saved, and the looks of the view can be improved as well. The sides of the object are developed on the third, or cross, axis and at an angle that best reveals the detail.

It may be impossible to avoid a circle in the side of an oblique drawing. If the circle is in the regular oblique plane, it can be approximated by the same method used with the isometric.

The complicated face that is placed parallel to the picture plane may have more than one surface. The starting plane under these conditions is a reference plane parallel to the picture plane and usually within the object. The frontal surfaces are developed by measuring offsets forward and back from the reference plane and in the angle of the cross axis.

The offset method is a convenient way to draw an object with an irregular surface in either the oblique or isometric drawings. The reference plane can be horizontal or vertical, and a series of offsets, or reference points, are measured perpendicularly from various positions on the plane.

To reduce the distortion and improve the looks of the oblique drawing, the draftsman sometimes uses a *cabinet* drawing. It is constructed with the complicated face parallel to the picture plane like the oblique, but the top and sides, or the distances measured parallel to the cross axis, are reduced in scale. The measurement may be reduced to the ratio of 1 to 2 for drafting convenience, although it makes the object look too thin. A ratio of 2 to 3 or 3 to 4 is often a more pleasing proportion. By always labeling the cabinet drawing and giving the ratio of the measurements on the cross axis, the possibility of its being mistaken for an oblique drawing is avoided.

44

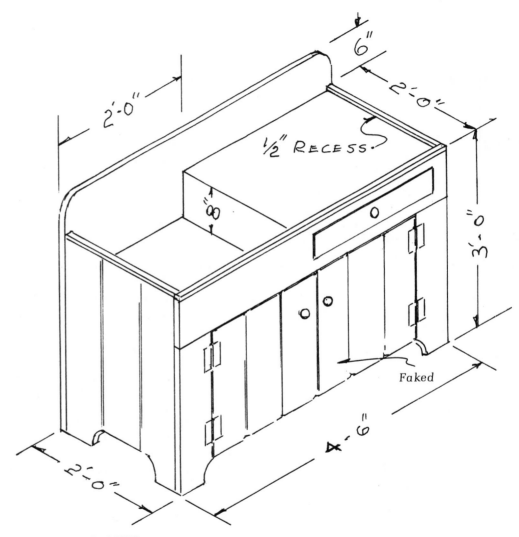

½" RECESS.

2'-0"

6"

2'-0"

3'-0"

8"

Faked

4'-6"

2'-0"

PINE DRY SINK
An example of a dimensioned isometric drawing. Many built properties and simple three-dimensional forms can be quickly presented in this manner.

9

Floor Plans

Long before starting the working drawings of a set, the importance of the floor plan is realized. A designer continually thinks of the plan while the idea of the setting is developed. The plan grew with the design, pushed one way for aesthetic reasons, altered another way for practical reasons, modified for staging reasons, and, finally, solidified into the key working drawing and information center—the *floor plan.*

To explain the design of his set adequately, the designer finds it necessary to refer often to the plan. The carpenter consults it to lay out the construction. The director and stage manager are unable to map out the staging without understanding and studying the plan. The setup, rigging, and lighting depend on information in the plan to complete the final assembly of the set on the stage.

As has been mentioned, the floor plan is a horizontal section with the cutting plane passed at a level that shows (when the upper portion of the set is removed) the most characteristic view of the shape of the set. Because a stage set is made up of many small units of scenery, the floor is also an assembled view. The floor plan, then, reveals the horizontal shape of the set, locates it on the stage, shows the scenery assembled, and identifies with labels the units and pieces that make up the complete set.

The floor plan is usually drawn at the scale of $\frac{1}{2}'' = 1'0''$. At this scale, it is necessary to use symbols and conventions to help explain the set with a limited amount of detailed drafting. Most of the symbols are familiar ones and the use and meanings are logical enough if it is kept in mind that a plan is a sectional view.

Inasmuch as the walls of the set, or units of scenery, are cut by the sectional view, they are drawn in a heavyweight section outline. The cross section of framed scenery is less than an inch; consequently, at small scale it is customary to represent it in plan as a solid black line rather than section outlines and crosshatching.

The heavy section outline of the wall is stopped at openings. If the opening is a door or archway, it is bridged with a dotted line indicating a *header* over the opening. A break in the section outline without the dotted lines is interpreted as a separated wall unit without a connecting header. A door can be identified quickly if it is drawn ajar with an arc and arrowhead to show the direction the door swings. The arc and arrowhead is a lightweight line and it can also be used to note

FLOOR PLAN SYMBOLS

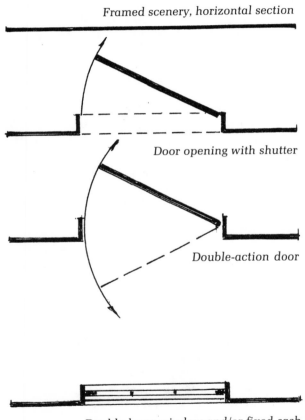

Framed scenery, horizontal section

Door opening with shutter

Double-action door

Double-hung window and/or fixed sash

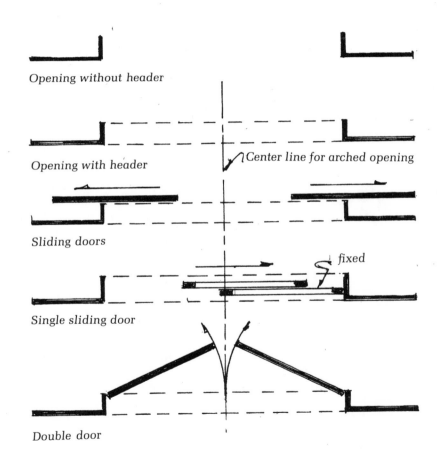

Opening without header

Opening with header

Center line for arched opening

Sliding doors

Single sliding door

fixed

Double door

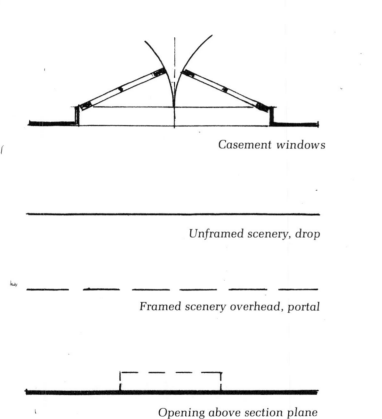

Casement windows

Unframed scenery, drop

Framed scenery overhead, portal

Opening above section plane

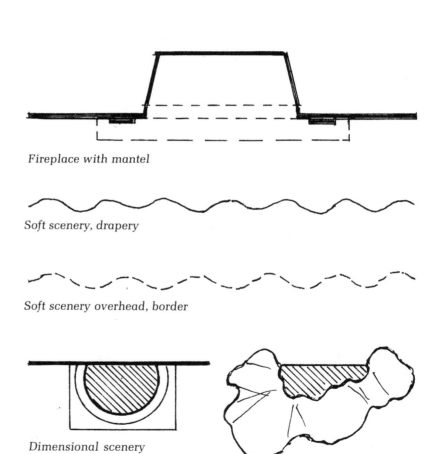

Fireplace with mantel

Soft scenery, drapery

Soft scenery overhead, border

Dimensional scenery

FLOOR PLAN SYMBOLS

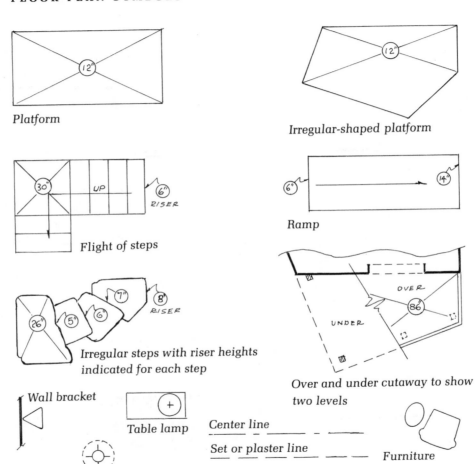

Platform

Irregular-shaped platform

Flight of steps

Ramp

Irregular steps with riser heights
indicated for each step

Over and under cutaway to show
two levels

Wall bracket

Table lamp

Center line

Chandelier lighting fixtures

Set or plaster line

Furniture

Reference lines

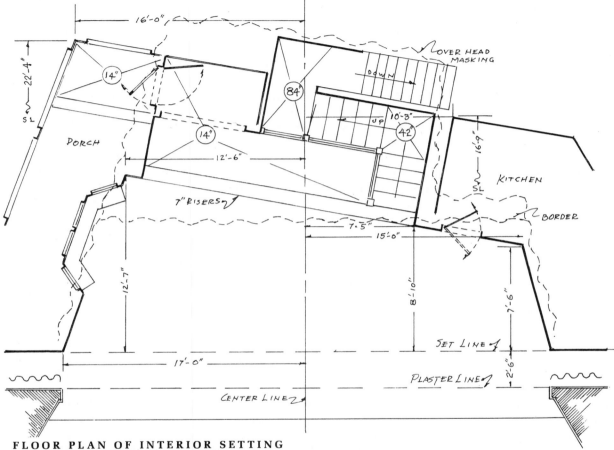

16'-0"

22'-4"

SL

OVER HEAD
MASKING

DOWN

PORCH

14"

14"

84"

42"

10'-3"

UP

12'-6"

16'-9"

SL

KITCHEN

BORDER

7" RISERS

7-5"

15'-0"

12'-7"

8'-10"

7'-6"

SET LINE

PLASTER LINE

2'-6"

17'-0"

CENTER LINE

FLOOR PLAN OF INTERIOR SETTING

Floor plan for shop and stage carpenter. Enough dimensions are given to locate set on the stage. Platform and riser heights are noted as well as overhead masking. Key reference lines are "center line" and "set line." Distance to plaster line would vary with the theatre. More information can be included such as labeling of units of scenery and spotting lines for hanging of masking.

the swing of casement windows, double doors, and moving, or "wild," portions of the set.

If the opening is a window, it is bridged with a solid medium-weight line. This is the window sill as it is viewed from above. A cornice or overhanging portion of scenery that is above the sectional view is noted with the medium-weight dashed line symbol for an adjacent part.

Steps, levels, and other objects below the cutting plane of the section are shown as a medium-weight visible outline. From above, the direction of a ramp or the elevation of steps is not apparent without a leader noting that the arrow is pointing up or down. A note stating the height of all risers is sufficient if the steps are regular. If riser heights are irregular, however, the height of each step should be given.

In a floor plan, the outline of levels and platforms sometimes becomes confused and lost in the rest of the set. It is good practice, therefore, to identify further the area of a level or change in height, by drawing in its diagonals. A notation of the height of a level from the stage floor is set into a circle, or balloon, that is drawn at the point where the diagonals cross.

The floor plan is dimensioned from two reference lines, the center line of the proscenium opening and the set line—a dashed line drawn from the right return to the left return to mark the downstage extremity of the set. It is not necessary to dimension the plan in great detail because all the scenery will appear in separate elevational views with complete dimensions. If it is kept in mind that the floor plan is also an assembled view, it will help to determine what dimension the stage carpenter needs to know to locate and assemble the set on the stage.

How wide are the tormentors? How deep is the back corner of the set? Distances to the left and right use the center line as a base line, while all depth measurements are taken directly or indirectly from the set line. Any point on the stage is located by its distance right or left of the center line and its measurement upstage from the set line. After all important corners and backings are located, a few additional dimensions may be needed, such as overall dimensions of a wall, a unit of scenery, and radius dimensions of circles, or arcs, that may be in the floor plan.

Part of the function of an assembled view is to identify and label the parts that make up the whole. The floor plan gives this information in varying degrees of completeness depending upon the working conditions and the nature of the show. In designing for summer stock and university and community theatres where the bulk of the structural planning falls on the designer's shoulders, he may want to be more specific in his labeling of each piece of scenery in the show.

The floor plan of a television show also contains a careful notation of each piece of scenery. Television scenery is almost entirely of stock units and standard sizes. The designer's labels and notes on the plan are a catalogue, or index guide, for assembling the set in the studio.

A simple box set can be broken down into wall units, such as left wall, back wall, right wall, hall backing, stairway wall, and so forth. If the divisions of the walls are obvious in the plan the units can be referred to with the same descriptive phrases rather than a number or letter system.

A show with many sets can become confusing especially if some of the scenery doesn't change or is altered and moved to a new position in the plan. Each unit of scenery is labeled to clarify the movement and alteration taking place in the floor plans as well as accounting for all the different units. To show this visually, a composite plan can be used by drawing the floor plans of the sets over each other in a composite view. Each set is given a different line symbol so the outline can be traced. It is a schematic plan and of little value as a working drawing. A composite plan's chief purpose is for showing and studying shifting problems, flying or rigging problems, and lighting problems, as well as showing the general interrelation of the sets. The carpenter will still want a separate floor plan with each set of elevation and working drawings.

Another type of schematic plan is the *furniture plot* used to locate the position of set properties in each scene. It is generally drawn at ¼ scale with furniture in position. The furniture plot is not dimensioned unless there is need to call attention to a certain measurement. It is drawn on a grid of 1' or 2' squares, so anyone can figure distances by counting squares. Such a plan is useful to the director and stage manager for laying out rehearsal space and studying the staging. It is valuable to the property man as a visual reference list of his set props. And the designer will find he can use it in planning the lighting of the production.

The floor plan of a television show is handled in essentially the same way. It is drawn at ¼ scale over a grid of 1' squares showing the set props in place as well as noting and numbering each piece of scenery.

On a very heavy show, a *hanging* plan may be needed to indicate the disposition of all the scenery that is to be flown. To keep the plan from becoming confusing, most of the scenery on the floor is not shown. The hanging plan may be very general and schematic or quite detailed, depending on the proportion of the rigging, the theatre, and type of show. For a wing and backdrop type of production, for example, it is little more than a listing of drops in the order they will hang and the numbering of the act and scene in which they will work.

Even a more complicated rigging plan will vary if the show is on the road. This is usually taken into consideration in the overall scheme of the sets. The floor plan is an open one with room to expand, or contract, according to the requirements of each theatre.

If a production is designed for one theatre in New York or—as occurs in civic repertory—community and university theatres, the hanging plan can be more specific within the limitations of one stage. Under these conditions, it is usually developed with a *hanging section* using a cross section of the stage and house. This takes the guesswork out of vertical masking. To locate borders and to determine ground row heights, vertical sight lines are drawn from the extreme seats in the house, these being the first row of the orchestra and the last row of the balcony.

Recent engineering developments in a more flexible flying system and gridiron design than the existing pin and rail and counterweight methods indicate a time in the future when the hanging plan will be a required drawing for every show.

Graphic Information for Lighting

As soon as the design and its floor plan have been solidified there are two necessary drawings that have to be prepared for the planning of the lighting. They are a floor plan or plans and related sectional views of the setting. If the setting is an interior, a plan showing furniture arrangement (p. 52) is very useful. An exterior setting or musical would require a basic plan of the masking (wings and borders) and a hanging plan of all units of scenery with the batten or line set numbers (p. 54).

The most important view for the lighting designer is a sectional view showing trim heights and hanging space. A typical cross section of the stage and a portion of the auditorium showing front-of-house lighting positions is a necessary drawing to figure the length-of-throw that helps to determine the intensity and beam spread

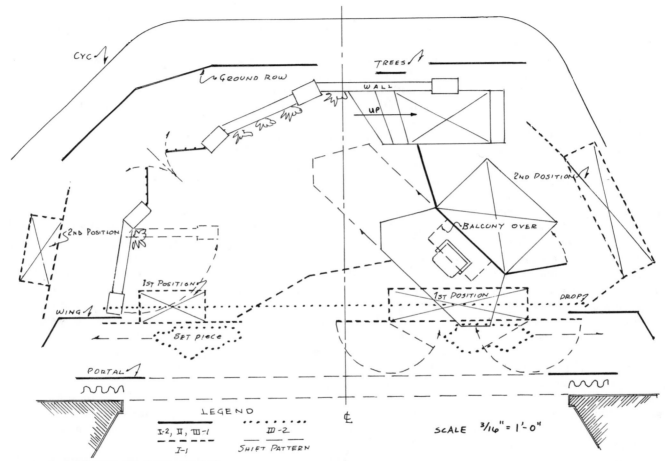

CYC

TREES

GROUND ROW

WALL

UP

2ND POSITION

BALCONY OVER

2ND POSITION

1ST POSITION

1ST POSITION

DROP?

WING

SET PIECE

PORTAL

LEGEND

I-2, II, III-1   • • • •   III-2

I-1   SHIFT PATTERN

¢

SCALE 3/16" = 1'-0"

COMPOSITE FLOOR PLAN

A schematic plan for the movement of scenery. An overlay of the plans of three settings
showing the working and stored position of elements of scenery within a basic set. A scaled
drawing without dimensions.

FLOOR PLAN

A lot of information has been worked into a single drawing. A floor plan with several levels and a moving unit is explained with over and under cutaways, enlarged details, and elevations of risers and levels.

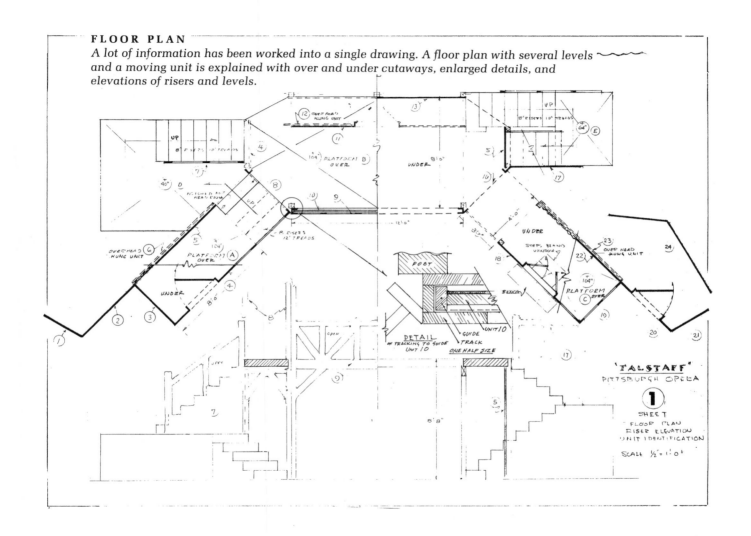

54

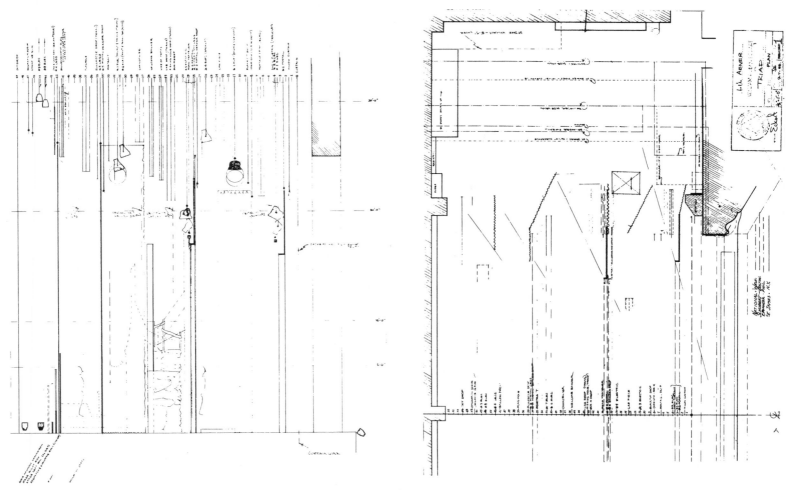

HANGING SECTION FOR *LIL ABNER*
Designed by Jean and William Eckart

STAGE-LEFT PORTION OF HANGING PLAN FOR *LIL ABNER*
Designed by Jean and William Eckart

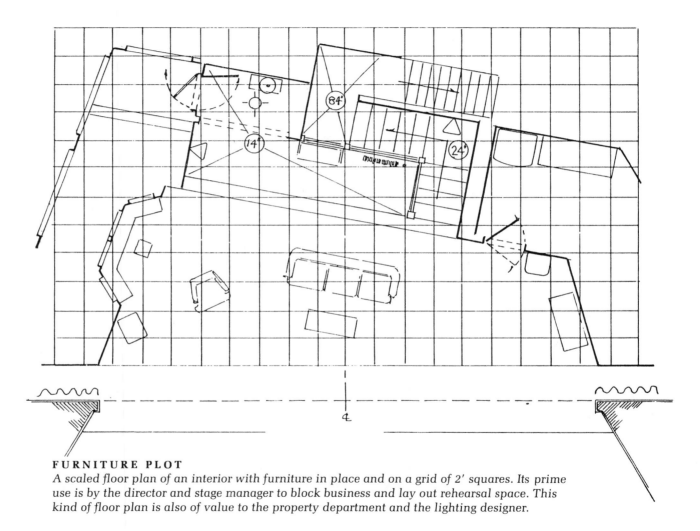

FURNITURE PLOT

A scaled floor plan of an interior with furniture in place and on a grid of 2' squares. Its prime use is by the director and stage manager to block business and lay out rehearsal space. This kind of floor plan is also of value to the property department and the lighting designer.

of the lighting instrument. The resulting lighting plot, however, will have little resemblance to these two views, for it is a diagram or plot, as the name suggests, and not a graphic representation.

Computer Assistance

The adaptation of computer graphics as a drafting aid is a rapidly advancing technique. Computer assistance has been successfully integrated into architectural drafting and can be easily adapted to drafting in the theatre. Although routine drafting is not always applicable, to draw a repeated structural element or foreshortened repetition of a decorative detail, computer graphics can save time and hasten decisions.

The use of a computer, however, does not replace the need of a knowledge and skill in drafting. It is still necessary to study drafting techniques and to be familiar with its symbols and conventions as well as the special requirements of the theatre.

It is obvious that the possession of computer hardware and programing by every producing theatre or scene designer is unrealistic. However, this was not a limiting factor in the printout illustrated on page

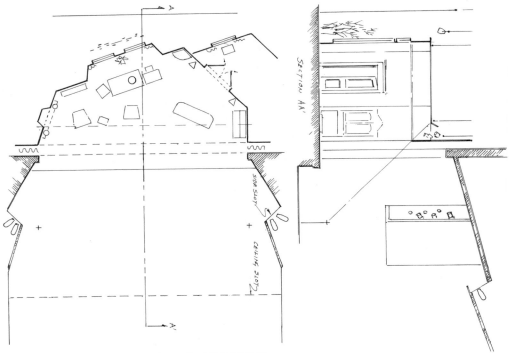

STAGE FLOOR PLAN AND SECTION
The alignment of the floor plan with sectional view indicates the method of developing a cross section of the stage and auditorium. Although they later become separate drawings, both are necessary for the planning of stage lighting.

61. In this example, the English National Opera, London, turned to an outside computer specialist to solve their problem with a minimum of cost and time. The printout was easily incorporated with the rest of the production drawings.

10

Elevations

Which comes first, the elevations or the floor plan? Should the plan be completed before starting the elevations, or vice versa? Although the floor plan and elevation are separate drawings and are sometimes at different scales, the safest way out of a prolonged discussion is to assume that they are developed simultaneously. This is true in most cases for there is a continual cross-reference between the plan and the elevation before either reaches its final form.

The term elevation applies to all views seen in a horizontal direction. A front view of the set is an elevation. Because the elevation of an assembled set has little value as a working drawing, the stage designer uses another technique. Compared to the floor plan, which is an assembled section showing the relation of the many parts, the elevation drawings are, in a sense, disassembled or dismantled views. The set is taken apart, flattened out, and each piece of scenery is shown in front view at a scale of $\frac{1}{2}'' = 1'0''$. Starting with the right return, the scenery is laid out in order, piece by piece, to the left return. All the pieces are shown in true size and shape.

A solid line marks open joints or edges between walls. In effect each flat wall surface or unit of scenery is an outline. The outline may include a large area involving a major portion of the scene or may merely mark off a small jog in the wall.

For special reasons, it may be necessary to indicate a covered joint, or the line, where two or more wings are hinged together to make up a flat wall surface. The covered joint is indicated with a dotted line and a note to hinge and to dutchman, or cover, the joint. Normally, this isn't necessary as the carpenter decides just how an oversized surface will be subdivided. His decision as to how it is to be made is guided by such technical considerations as the size of the stage, the method of handling the sets, and if the scenery has to be transported, the nature of the transportation. The standard maximum wing width of 5′9″ is based on the height of a baggage car door. If the scenery is moving by truck, or not traveling at all, the maximum standard width can vary accordingly.

Designers vary in the amount of detail they show at ½″ scale. Although the decorative trim and other details are better shown at a larger scale, it is sometimes wise to at least sketch a portion of the detail on the ½″ elevations. It not only shows the trim in assembled view but also gives the carpenter some idea of any special construction that might be needed. Because of the light wood frame and canvas

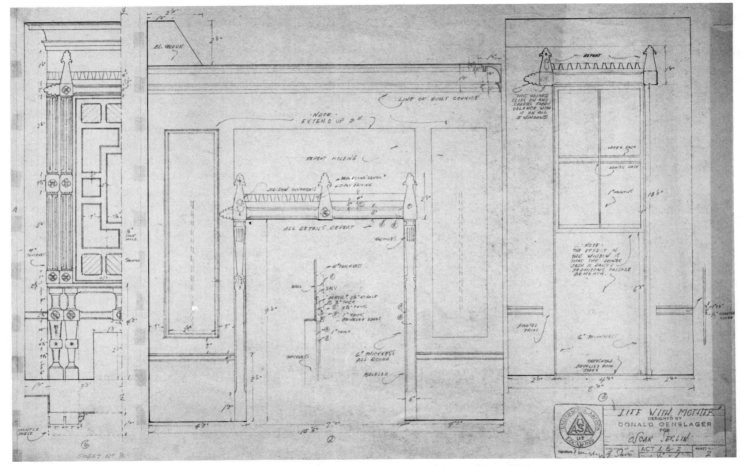

A portion of the designer's elevations for Life with Mother, designed by Donald Oenslager. Note
the indication of all applied details, such as trim, cornice, mouldings, and picture battens.
Also shown is an assembled view of the fireplace.

Elevations for the scenic artists are developed in two categories. First, the cartoon, or line drawing, supplying the artist with a layout of the design. It may or may not be gridded with 2' squares for scale reference, as some scenic artists prefer to plan their own grids.

SCALE ½" = 1'-0"

PAINTER'S ELEVATIONS 2
The second elevation provides the artist with the complete design indicating color and painting techniques. Between the two drawings of this cut drop the artist has information pertaining to layout, open spaces, translucent and opaque areas, color, and techniques.

construction of scenery, pictures, valance boxes, or lighting fixtures can't be placed in the middle of a wall without providing extra structural support from behind. If the applied details are partially sketched in the elevation, or indicated with the dashed line symbol of an adjacent part, the carpenter will know where to supply the additional construction.

Labeling

Obviously, the labeling of the elevation must agree with the labels of the corresponding units of the plan. The accuracy of cross-labeling is especially important when stock scenery is being used, for unless the set is extremely simple, it is the carpenter's only guide as to how the pieces assemble. On occasions, for clarification, a portion of a floor plan may be repeated near the elevation drawings of a complicated unit of scenery. The practice of careful labeling is not only helpful to the carpenter but also provides the designer and scenic artist with a method of accounting for every unit of scenery to be painted.

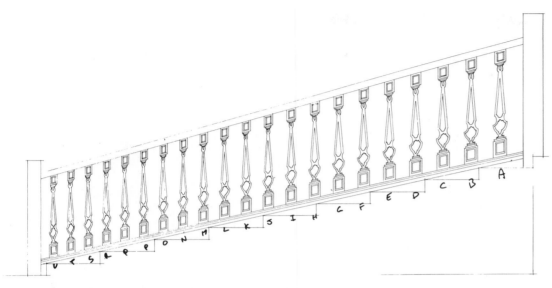

COMPUTER AIDS TO DRAFTING
Elevation of a stair railing descending through the stage floor to a lower level. The computer was supplied with a scaled drawing of a balustrade (A). The number of balustrades, overall distance, and vanishing point were also specified. The computer spaced and reduced the image of (A) into this foreshortened elevation. Each balustrade was then photo-enlarged to full scale to serve as a pattern for the carpenter. Courtesy Noel Stanton, Technical Director, English National Opera, Coliseum, London.

Notes

Scenery elevations also need notes on the types of material and the action, or business required of a portion of a set. If the construction departs from the traditional wood frame and canvas, the carpenter needs more information. It is not necessary to design the construction, but a note, for example, stating that a platform must be strong enough to support eight-dancing-girls-eight, or that a windowsill is to hold a one-hundred-pound statue of grandfather gives the carpenter an idea of the strength of material and construction that is needed.

The dimensions of the elevations, as well as being clearly placed, accurate, and complete, can be of greater use if finished dimensions are given. A finished dimension is the outside measurements of an object when it is finished, or the inside measurements of a window or door as it is to look when it is finished. The carpenter will determine the construction allowances and tolerances. The designer may, however, set maximum limits on a tolerance of a door, window, or moving part if he thinks too loose a fit affects the design.

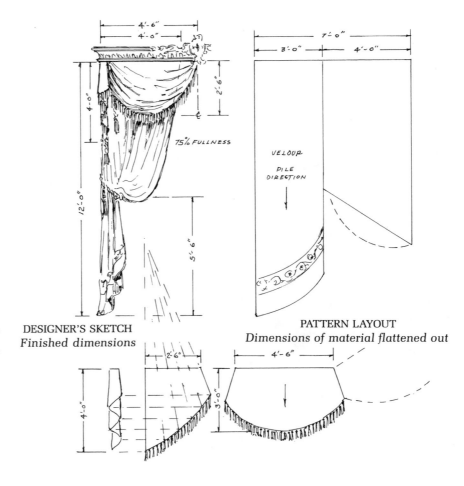

DESIGNER'S SKETCH
Finished dimensions

PATTERN LAYOUT
Dimensions of material flattened out

DRAPERY DETAILS
A designer's sketch drawn to scale, or dimensioned, is enough information for a professional drapery house. If it is a do-it-yourself production the pattern layout becomes important.

Details

Because the plan and elevations are often drafted at ½″ scale, small details may be lost and need to be enlarged for clarification. Normally such details as door trim, cornice, tricky construction, or assembly are drawn at 1″ scale for a more graphic definition. Very important information, however, is drawn at full scale or actual size.

Decorative details such as window draperies also require elevations. A professional drapery house works best from an elevation drawing of the drapes as they are to look in position. Along with a careful drawing the designer specifies the quality and weight of fabric. This affects the way the curtain hangs, or drapes, and the amount of light it transmits. The specifications also include notes on color, degree of fullness, and a description of the action, for a curtain may draw or tableau, or a swag may have to unfold.

If the curtains are going to be made with unskilled help, the drawings have to contain construction details, such as type and direction of seams, direction of materials, depth of hem, and patterns for cutting the more difficult swags. This information is given on a sketch of the un-

DRAPERY ELEVATIONS

Drapery elevations for the period interior, A Doll's House, are collected on one sheet. Valances, overdrapes, and glass curtains are drawing at 1″ scale for the convenience of the property department.

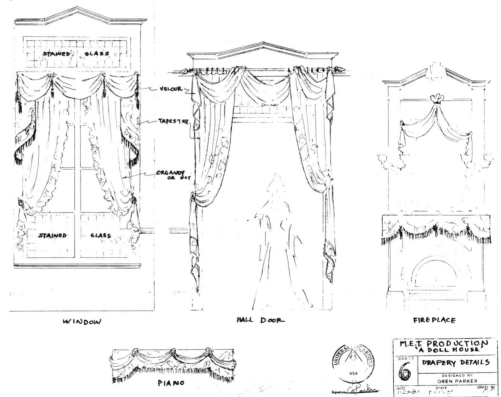

finished drape showing the material flat as it looks before sewing in the fullness or swags.

Compositional Elevations

Borrowing a trick from the interior decorator, the stage designer sometimes uses a *compositional* elevation. It works best on an interior setting, for it is an assembled view of each wall with all the set dressings related to that wall in place. In this manner, the designer can study the composition of the furniture, pictures, and window drapes at a reduced scale. He is able to make decisions on the sizes of properties and pictures during that hectic stage of combining all the elements that make up an interior. A compositional elevation is usually drawn at ¼″ scale, or smaller, and any jogs, or breaks, in the wall are not flattened out but are shown in position.

By working on graph paper, the necessity of using dimensions is eliminated and a simple method of calculating sizes and proportions is provided. It can be seen that this kind of drawing is in no way a working drawing for the carpenter but is of value to the designer himself, his drafting assistant, and set dresser.

It is equally important for the designer not only to be able to draft his own show but also to know how to turn over adequate information to an assistant if someone else is doing the drafting. A carefully drawn set of compositional elevations and a floor plan provide such information. The designer will also find that, next to a scaled model, this is an excellent way to explain an interior setting to the director and stage manager in a simple use of the language of lines.

Technical Drafting

Although the designer is usually not involved with construction of scenery or technical drafting there may be occasions when this skill is required. If the design, for example, is going to be built with unskilled hands, as in the case in many community and university theatres, the designer becomes the chief guardian of the construction. To avoid being tied to shop supervision at a time that could be better spent selecting props, preparing painters elevations, and doing countless other chores, it pays to make a set of construction drawings.

Technical drafting evolves into three different types of drawings related to the structural form of the unit of scenery. Technical drafting is equally concerned with the framing of flat scenery, the internal structure of three-dimensional scenery, and the isolated drawing of a mechanical or structural detail.

The simplest way to lay out framing construction is to use *rear* elevations. A view from this direction looks at the scenery as it appears under construction in the shop. A rear elevation shows the framing and profiling, explains the assembly, locates the hinges, and indicates bracing and stiffening. The detail and completeness of the rear elevations can be gauged by the aptitude of the shop help. An experienced stage carpenter might need a construction drawing for the occasional unusual piece of scenery, while inexperienced help would need every piece of scenery detailed. The knowledge of drafting symbols to simplify the drawings of the *framing, joining, bracing,* and *rigging* of framed scenery improves the ability to read and draft rear elevations.

Three-dimensional pieces, such as fireplaces, doors, steps, and rocks require more than just the designer's front elevations. At least a side view and often a sectional view are included. The sectional view not only shows the internal structure but helps to explain the contour of

COMPOSITIONAL ELEVATIONS

Compositional elevations are drawn to ⅛″ scale by Donald Oenslager for acts 1 and 2 of Life
with Mother. A surprising amount of detail is represented at a very small scale.

the object. Irregular forms, of course, may require many sections. Very special shapes, or profiles, many times are drawn at full scale to serve as a pattern.

Construction details are occasionally shown in full scale to ensure correct dimensions and space allowance. A typical cross section, such as the example illustrated, serves as a guide for accurate construction and assembly.

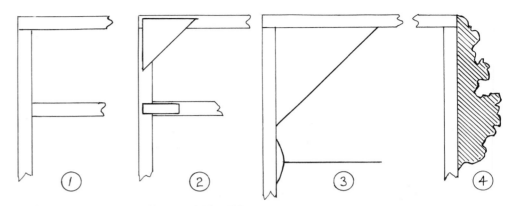

TECHNICAL DRAFTING SYMBOLS

Flat scenery framing or rear elevation: 1) framing layout; 2) keystone and corner blocks; 3) brace and toggle rail; 4) change of material.

TECHNICAL DRAFTING SYMBOLS   *Framed scenery joining techniques and hardware: 5) tight pin hinge (below); TPH on opposite face; 6) loose pin hinge (below); LPH on opposite face; 7) stop block; 8) stop cleat; 9) lash line in corner block; 11) lash eye.*

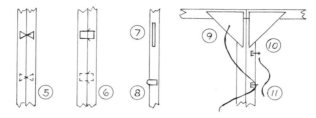

Stiffening and bracing framed scenery: 12) loose pin stiffener (horizontal 1 × 3 on edge); 13) stage brace cleat; 14) keeper hook; 15) vertical LPH brace or folding jack.

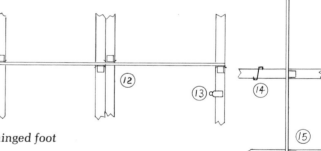

Rigging framed scenery to hang: 16) top hanger iron; 17) bottom hanger iron; 18) hinged foot iron; 19) rigid foot iron; 20) ceiling plate; 21) picture hook and socket.

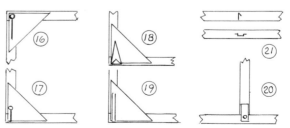

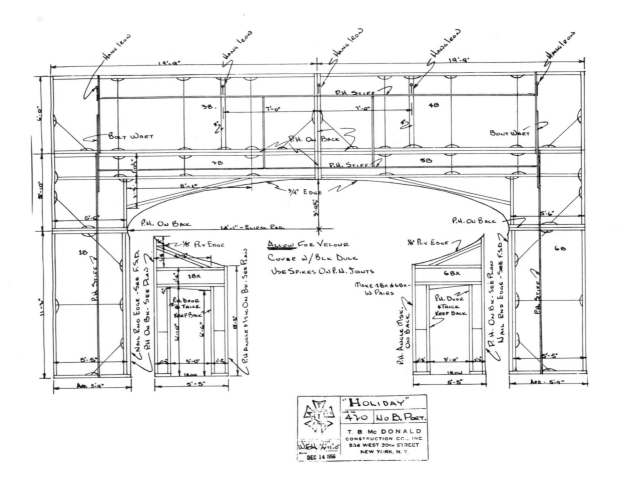

Layout drawings, from T. B. McDonald Construction Company, showing the framing of a show portal. Notice that the drawing has been simplified by using a symbol for the shoe and rail assembly, which is understood by the carpenters. Less experienced help would need more construction details.

TYPICAL CROSS SECTION

A full-scale sectional view of a stagewagon assembly. Shown in the view is the top (1), framing (2), caster plank (3), and the caster (4). Although the facing (5) appears in this view, it is, of course, not typical for all edges of the wagon.

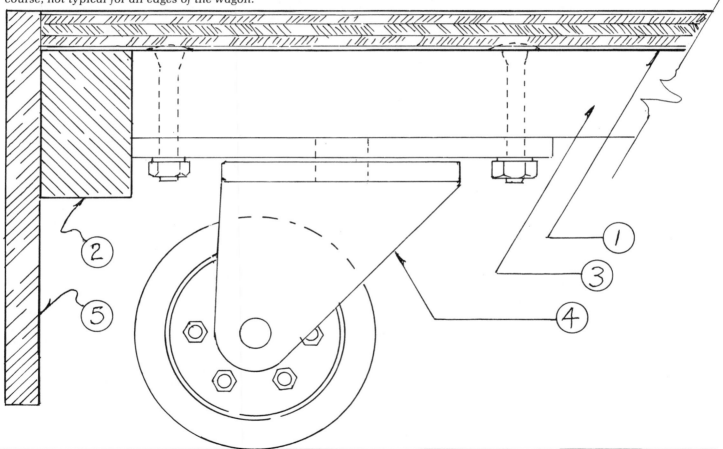

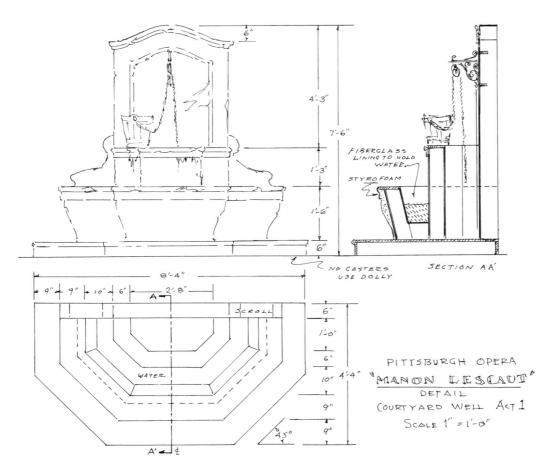

6"

4'-3"

7'-6"

1'-3"

1'-6"

6"

FIBERGLASS
LINING TO HOLD
WATER.

STYROFOAM

NO CASTERS
USE DOLLY

SECTION AA'

8'-4"

9" 9" 10" 6" 2'-8"

A

SCROLL

6"

1'-0"

6"

WATER

10" 4'-4"

9"

45°

9"

A'

PITTSBURGH OPERA
"MANON LESCAUT"
DETAIL
COURTYARD WELL ACT 1
SCALE 1" = 1'-0"

THREE-DIMENSIONAL SCENERY

The construction drawings for three-dimensional units of scenery that do not "knock down" into smaller or flat units are many times best explained by sectional views and the dimensions of principal surfaces in the front and top view. A rear elevation is of limited value.

Part Two   Graphic Solutions

11

Space Patterns

As the designer's elevational drawings are prepared, it may be difficult to show certain distorted walls or angled pieces of scenery in true size and shape. Most of these unusual pieces can be reasoned out with common sense and visual imagination. Occasionally, however, there are shapes that defy all solutions and the designer wishes he had an extra trick up his sleeve. The draftsman has a few tricks that every scene designer should know, not only to develop the elevation of a box set, but to help find the true size and shape of any distorted piece of scenery, platform, or three-dimensional object.

In a sense, the average interior setting is a partially closed solid, and the designer's elevations are a scaled pattern of the solid unfolded from the inside. The draftsman refers to these patterns as *developments*. Most of the surfaces in scenery are *plane surfaces* bounded by straight lines and are easy to develop. A plane surface, when angled, is usually perpendicular to at least one of the three principal planes of projection. The resulting perpendicular projection or *edge view* reveals the true angle of the plane. Problems arise when a plane surface is *askew* or angled to all three principal planes of projection.

Although an askew plane is a complexity of plane surfaces, often a piece of scenery may be further complicated by containing curved surfaces. A curved surface may be based on a single curve or a double curve that can limit it as a developable surface. Many *single-curved surfaces* can be developed; however, some have warped surfaces that can only be approximated. *Double-curved surfaces* such as the sphere cannot be developed or, at best, only crudely approximated. And of course, *irregular surfaces* or free forms cannot be developed at all.

By now it can be seen that to be able to analyze the surface and structure of a solid it is going to be necessary to become familiar with many geometric shapes. So back to geometry to review some of the planes and solids that frequently occur in scenery. A basic knowledge of geometric structure helps to tell at a glance how to develop a solid or whether it can be developed at all.

12

Surfaces

A regular surface can be defined as the path of a moving line. If the line is straight it is known as a *ruled surface*. The line that moves to generate a surface is the *generatrix* and in any one the generatrix is known as an *element*. The movement of the generatrix, to generate a surface, may be in any direction except in a straight line, like an arrow.

The simplest ruled surface is a *plane* that can be described several ways. For example, two parallel lines form a plane, as do two intersecting lines. A line segment rotating about one of its ends forms a plane. Any enclosed area forms a plane, such as triangles or any polygon by definition. To be concise, a plane is present when two elements are *parallel* or *intersect*.

A solid may either be formed by combining planes or generated from a single-curved line. A *single-curved surface* occurs when the generatrix, a straight line, is guided or directed by a single-curved line, called the *directrix*. A single-curved surface, such as the cone or the cylinder, can be developed. A cylinder may have a variety of shapes dependent upon the shape and position of the curved-line directrix. When the directrix is a circle and the elements revolve parallel to the center axis, the cylinder is known as a *right cylinder*.

PLANE

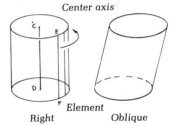

Line AB rotating about A

Parallel lines

Intersecting lines

CYLINDER

Center axis

Element

Right

Oblique

CONE

Right

Oblique

OH: Center axis
OG: Element

A *right cone* is generated when the elements revolve about the axis making a constant angle with the axis. The directrix, of course, is a circle. Cones, other than right cones, vary with the shape of the directrix and the location of the vertex. An oblique cone, for example, may have an offset vertex and a directrix elliptical in shape.

In relation to the cone it is interesting to note that most of the common geometric curves are *conic sections*. By cutting a right circular cone with planes at different angles, four types of curves are obtained, any one of which may appear as a directrix for a single- or double-curved surface. These are the *circle*, by a horizontal cut with a plane perpendicular to the axis; the *ellipse*, by a cutting plane making a greater angle to the axis than the elements; the *parabola*, by a cutting plane with the same angle as the element; and the *hyperbola*, by a cutting plane making a smaller angle than the elements. Conic sections serve to illustrate the basic characteristics of the four geometric curves, which, of course, may be constructed more accurately by mathematical equations.

Cylinder sections also produce single-curved lines, but a more important double-curved line is found on the surface of the cylinder. The *helix* is a line

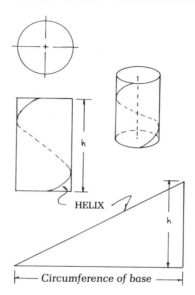

HELIX

Circumference of base

CONIC SECTIONS

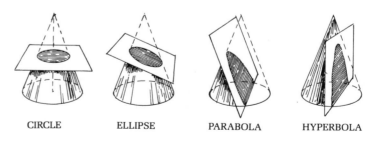

CIRCLE   ELLIPSE   PARABOLA   HYPERBOLA

generated by a point moving around an axis and parallel to the axis at the same time. One revolution would produce a *right-hand cylindrical helix.* The use of the helix in machinery is evident in the screw thread and worm gear.

The helix appears in scenery as the guiding line of a curved ramp or staircase, both of which are, in a sense, oversized segments of the screw thread. A curved ramp is a warped surface known as a *helicoid.* It is generated by a straight line moving about a cylinder, touching the helix, and maintaining a constant angle with axis. The helicoid, although theoretically impossible to develop, can be approximated either by warping a small area of the surface if made of plywood or by reducing the ramp to a series of small planes.

It is possible to combine plane surfaces so as to form solids of a similar shape to the cylinder and cone. The pyramid, for example, resembles the cone, and the prism has a likeness to the cylinder. Some hybrid surfaces occur from the crossing of these two types of solids. The result is a warped surface that though undevelopable can be approximated. The *transition piece* is a notable example of such a combination where the base or one end may be a square, while the top or opposite end is a circle. The shape is partly

WARPED SURFACES

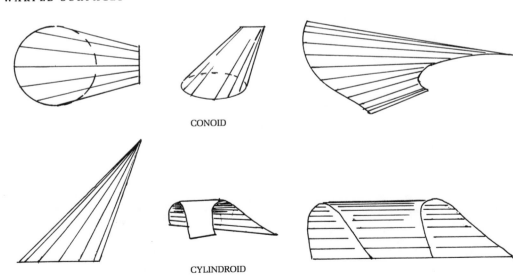

CONOID

CYLINDROID

plane surface and partly generated by a straight line.

Other warped surfaces related to the cone and cylinder are the *conoid* and the *cylindroid*. These two surfaces cannot be developed and have limited use in the theatre in terms of conventional scenery. They bear mentioning, however, so as to be recognized as undevelopable surfaces. This does not preclude their use in the theatre, for they may appear

in the sculptural free form of a three-dimensional piece of scenery where pliable materials are employed to form the warped surface. Such pieces usually remain three-dimensional and are never reduced to plane surfaces.

The warped surface of the conoid is generated by the movement of a straight-line element that is guided by a curved-line directrix at one end and a straight-line directrix at the other end. The cylindroid is

generated by a straight line that moves so as to touch two curved-line directrices while remaining parallel to a given plane. The two curved-line directrices are not in the plane of the straight line.

Two additional warped surfaces that are unrelated to the cylinder and cone but are still in the ruled surface group are the *hyperboloid* and the *hyperbolic paraboloid*. Their shapes are easier to describe than to spell. Again these are surfaces

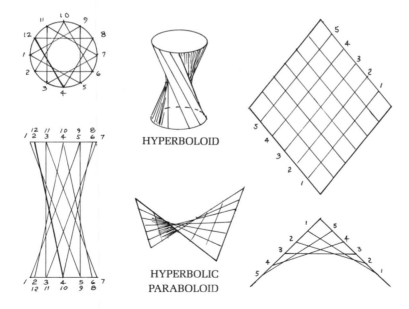

HYPERBOLOID

HYPERBOLIC
PARABOLOID

seldom appearing in scenery except possibly as a decorative use of open framing where the structure becomes a part of the design. In any event the solid cannot be reduced to flat planes.

A *hyperboloid* is generated by a straight line revolving about an axis to which it remains nonparallel and nonintersecting. A section containing the axis will be a hyperbola, while a section perpendicular to the axis will be a circle.

A hyperbolic paraboloid is the surface generated by the movement of a straight line that is guided by two straight-line directrices that are neither parallel nor intersecting. If the positions of the two directrices are not too askew to each other the resulting surface can be approximated.

The remaining geometric shapes are classed as *double-curved surfaces,* which means they are generated by the movement of a curved-line, rather than a straight-

line, element. Like the warped surfaces, they cannot be developed. In some cases, however, by reducing the curved surfaces into a series of flat planes, the solid can be approximated.

The *sphere* is the most familiar double-curved surface. It is formed by a circle revolving about its diameter. The circle can also be guided by lines other than its own diameter. It can be revolved about another circle, creating the *torus* or ring, or it can

DOUBLE-CURVED SURFACES

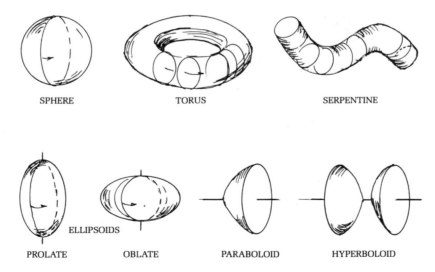

SPHERE   TORUS   SERPENTINE

ELLIPSOIDS

PROLATE   OBLATE   PARABOLOID   HYPERBOLOID

be revolved about a spiral or helix and produce a serpentine shape.

The other geometric lines, such as the ellipse, parabola, and hyperbola, can be revolved in the same manner to produce related shapes. The ellipse revolving about its major axis is known as an *ellipsoid* (*prolate*), while a revolution about its minor axis is known as an *ellipsoid* (*oblate*). The paraboloid is shaped by a parabola revolving about a symmetrical axis through its focus, and the *hyperboloid* by the hyperbola revolving about an axis through both foci.

13

True Length and Shape

The development of a full-size pattern of a surface, such as the patterns used in sheet-metal work, is infrequent in the theatre. Most of the surfaces are too large to be developed at full scale. Also, because most curved surfaces in scenery are not structural themselves, it is occasionally necessary to use full-scale lofting to find the true size and shape of the structural member that is supporting the curved surface rather than to find a pattern of the surface itself. Angled planes are worked out at full scale in the same manner or at a large scale on the drafting board.

The graphic solution of any true-size-and-shape problem involves the use and understanding of two basic descriptive geometry concepts. Most problems in the theatre can be solved by knowing how to *rotate a line* to show it in true length and angle and by understanding the process of developing a shape by *triangulation*.

The auxiliary view is, of course, another way to solve for true length and shape. It works best on small objects or portions of a setting. Because askew planes in scenery are usually large in size and often not complete objects, the rotation method provides an accurate solution with the least amount of additional drawing.

Finding the true length of a line, like any graphic solution, begins with the in-formation provided in two or more views or projections of the line and their relationship to the *folding line*. The folding line (FL), which represents the intersection of the vertical and horizontal planes of projection, is omitted though understood in the normal orthographic projection. It is easier, however, to show a line segment or single plane in space if the folding line is indicated with the conventional reference line symbol.

The draftsman can recognize a line parallel to one of the principal planes of projection by noting whether one of the line's projections is parallel to the folding line or not. When one projection of the line is parallel to FL the opposite view is seen in true length (TL). Similarly, if the top and front views are perpendicular to FL, the side view of the line is in true length. When a line is askew to all the principal planes of projection it has to be rotated into a parallel position with one of the planes to solve for true length.

1. With the line segment AB as an example, it is evident from its top and front view that it is askew in space and not parallel to either the vertical or horizontal plane of projection. Working in the top view, it is possible to rotate B to a position parallel to (FL) by using A as a center and AB as the radius of the arc.

2. The new position of B brings the line

TOP VIEW   FRONT VIEW   SIDE

AB: *Parallel to horizontal plane; top view true length.*
CD: *Parallel to vertical plane;* front *view true length.*
EF: *Parallel to profile plane; side* view *true length.*

AB parallel to (FL) and in no way changes the characteristic of the line. To bring the front view of line AB into agreement with its newly rotated position means finding the new location of B in front view. As the characteristic of the line was not changed, B is at the same elevation and must be directly below the top view of its new position. When this point is located and a line drawn from A to B, the top and front views now show line AB to be parallel to the vertical plane of projection. The opposite view or front view now reveals line AB in true length and true angle.

3. The rotation of a line may also take place in the front view to produce a true length in the top view.

Likewise, it may be desirable to develop a true length in the side view by rotating the top or front view of the line into a position perpendicular to (FL).

The graphic solution for true length of a line opens the way to find the true length of all the sides of an askew plane and reconstruct it in true size and shape. It is soon discovered, however, that to know all the sides of a quadrilateral or polygon is not enough. The sides may be put together at many different angles. This is true of all polygons but it is not true of the triangle. The angles of a tri-

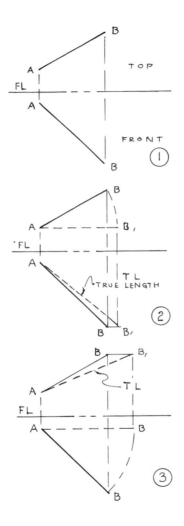

angle are predetermined by the length of its sides. If the true length of each side of a triangle is known it can be constructed by *triangulation*.

To demonstrate triangulation, triangle ABC is shown askew in space. The true length of each side is found by the rotation method. The side BC is drawn outside the drawing. At B an arc is swung using the true length of side AB as a radius. The process is repeated at C using an arc the length of side A. Where the two arcs cross is the point of intersection of the sides AB and AC. The triangle is completed by drawing the sides AB and AC to the intersection point. This is the only shape the triangle ABC can assume.

Any polygon can be reduced to a series of triangles by the addition of temporary diagonals. Each triangle is solved for true size by triangulation and combined with the next triangle to erect the true size and shape of the polygon.

The quadrilateral ABCD shown below, which might very easily be the top and front view of a shed or porch roof in an exterior setting, is an askew plane. Neither view shows the plane in its true size or shape. The true shape, which must be shown by the designer in painter's elevations and working drawings, is found in the steps below.

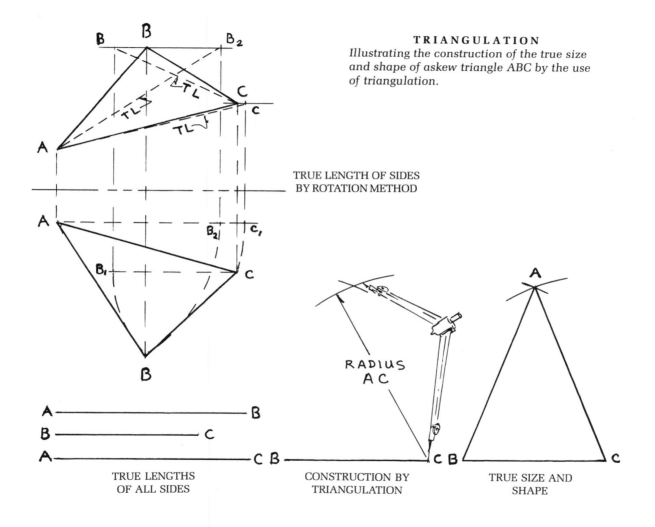

TRIANGULATION
*Illustrating the construction of the true size
and shape of askew triangle ABC by the use
of triangulation.*

TRUE LENGTH OF SIDES
BY ROTATION METHOD

TRUE LENGTHS
OF ALL SIDES

CONSTRUCTION BY
TRIANGULATION

TRUE SIZE AND
SHAPE

RADIUS
A C

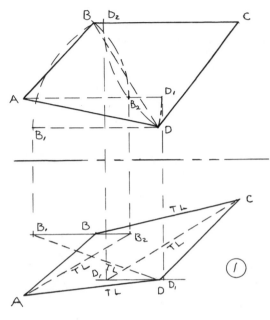

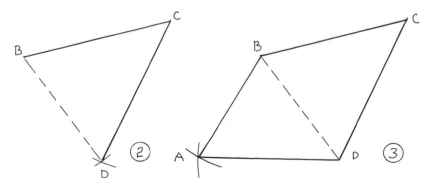

1. The true length of each side is found by the rotation method. Note that side BC is present in TL. Also, the temporary diagonal BD is rotated into a TL view.
2. Beginning with side BC, sides CD and temporary diagonal BD are attached by triangulation.
3. The final true shape is formed when the remaining sides BA and AD are located, also by triangulation, to complete the quadrilateral.

Developments

Many scenery surfaces are plane surfaces usually oriented to the stage floor and therefore easy to develop. The simple solid illustrated below is formed of five different plane surfaces. By unfolding these planes its pattern or development is shown in one plane. Like scenery this object is sitting upright on a base making the development simple because all edges appear in true dimension or can be easily found.

If this solid is a unit of scenery, however, there would be an important difference in the pattern although the thinking is the same. Because scenery surfaces have a front and back, the sides, top, and bottom as shown would have to be reversed to present the front face. Any symmetrically shaped surface is, of course, reversible.

As was mentioned earlier, the development of single-curved surfaces has limited uses in the theatre. Single-curved surfaces may appear in properties or small units of scenery, but seldom as the basis of a full setting. Some notable exceptions might be the lighthouse in *Thunder Rock* (segment of a circular cone) and the tent in *JB* (portion of a conic shaped top and cylindrical side walls).

DEVELOPMENT: PLANE SURFACES

1. *Top and front view of a truncated triangular prism.*
2. *Pictorial drawing showing the unfolding process of the prism's development.*
3. *Pattern or development of the prism. Note from the labeling how various dimensions and shapes are related to each other.*

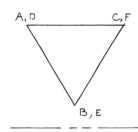

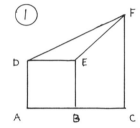

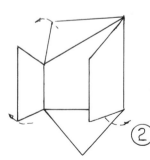

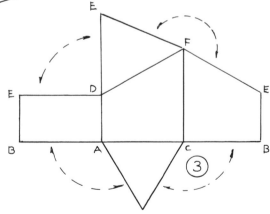

DEVELOPMENT: RIGHT TRIANGULAR PYRAMID

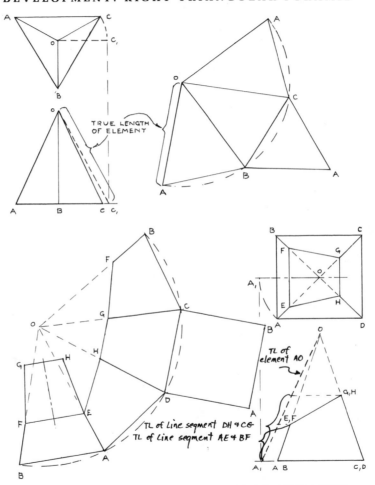

TRUE LENGTH OF ELEMENT

TL of element AO

TL of Line segment DH & CG
TL of Line segment AE & BF

TRUNCATED RIGHT RECTANGULAR PYRAMID

It is wise, however, to know the process of developing a single-curved surface, first, to better know the surface and, second, to know how to evolve the shape of the structural member that supports it.

The simplest single-curved surface is found in the right circular cylinder and cone. Both are developed by plotting selected positions of the element generating the surface. The pattern of the cylinder is formed by moving the element sideways over a distance equal to the circumference of the base or top. The cone is developed by rotating the element through an arc equal to the circumference of the base.

DEVELOPMENT: SINGLE-CURVED SURFACES

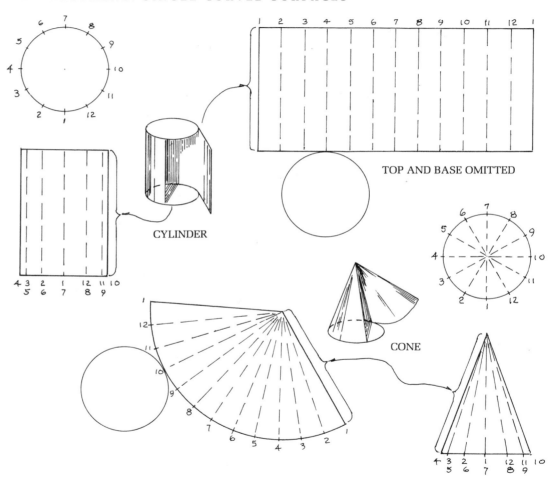

TOP AND BASE OMITTED

CYLINDER

CONE

14

Examples

DESIGNING FROM ELEVATION AND PLAN

1. *Elevation of left roof drawn to suit design with a temporary plan.*
2. *Misalignment of crossed diagonals indicates plan does not agree with elevation.*
3. *Elevation is held and plan is made to agree by constructing new diagonals.*
4. *Crossed diagonals of right roof and new plan do not align.*
5. *New plan is held and elevation of right roof is altered to agree.*
6. *Final step: Find true size and shape of each roof unit.*

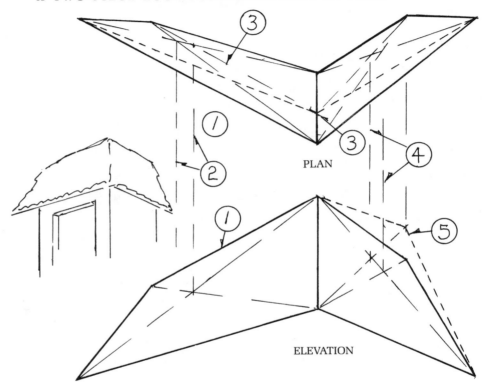

PLAN

ELEVATION

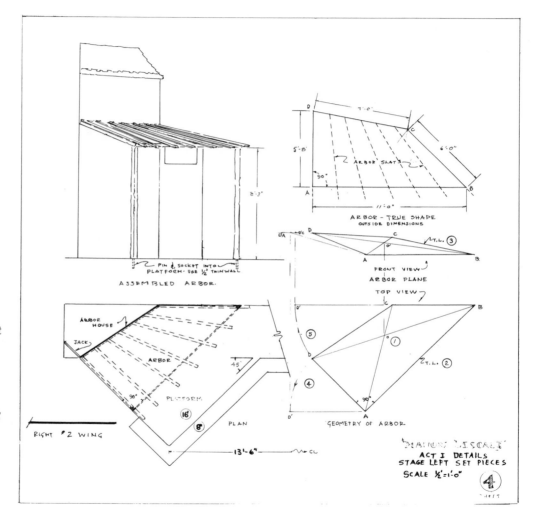

ARBOR - TRUE SHAPE
OUTSIDE DIMENSIONS

FRONT VIEW
ARBOR PLANE

TOP VIEW

ASSEMBLED ARBOR.

PIN & SOCKET INTO
PLATFORM - USE ½" THINWALL

GEOMETRY OF ARBOR

RIGHT #2 WING

PLAN

ACT I DETAILS
STAGE LEFT SET PIECES
SCALE ½"=1'-0"

GRAPHIC SOLUTION

Drafting example of finding the true size and shape of an askew plane of an assembled set piece. Shown at the left are the plan and assembled elevation of an arbor. At the right is the geometry of the arbor plane showing the steps of the solution. 1) Vertical alignment of the centers of crossed diagonals verify plane ABCD. 2) AB is seen in true length (TL) in top view. 3) TL of BC in front view. 4) DA is rotated around A to D', parallel to groundline. D'A in front view is TL. 5) In like manner D is rotated around C in top view. D'C is TL in front view. Above right, true lengths are assembled. AD and AB can be plotted using the right angle of the plane. The intersection of DC and BC by swing TL arcs of each side thereby forming the true size and shape of the arbor.

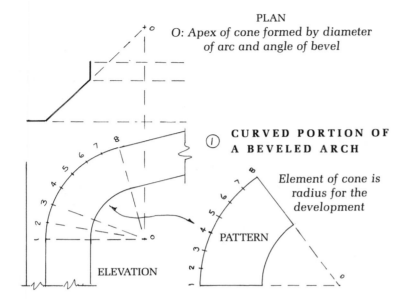

PLAN
O: *Apex of cone formed by diameter of arc and angle of bevel*

① **CURVED PORTION OF A BEVELED ARCH**

Element of cone is radius for the development

PATTERN

ELEVATION

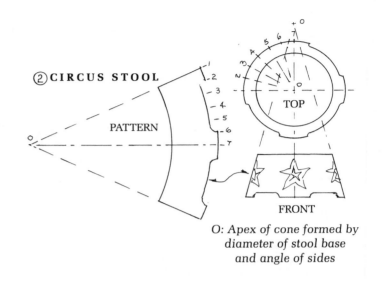

② **CIRCUS STOOL**

PATTERN

TOP

FRONT

O: *Apex of cone formed by diameter of stool base and angle of sides*

SEGMENTS OF CONIC SURFACES IN SCENERY AND PROPERTIES

SINGLE-CURVED SURFACE IN SCENERY: CUPOLA ROOF

BO PATTERN

Problem: Find the true curve of the structural member BO.

Given: Top and front view of roof showing true section at YO.

1) YO, typical section, is arbitrarily subdivided. 2) Subdivision spacing is produced to intersect top view of BO. 3) The extended spacing in the top view of BO is laid out and correlated with the front view spacing of BO. 4) The horizontal and vertical intersections of each point plot the true curve of each structural member.

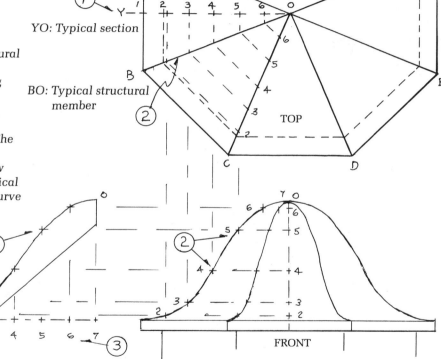

YO: Typical section

BO: Typical structural member

TOP

FRONT

15

Problems

Supply missing lines.

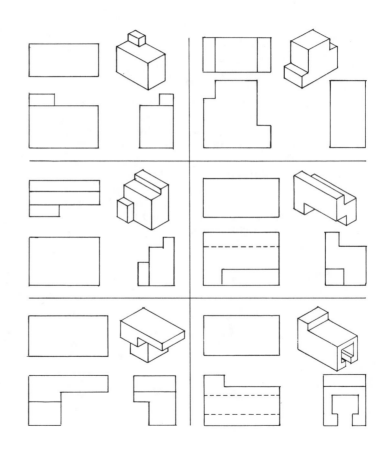

Problem 2. Orthographic Projections

Construct missing view.

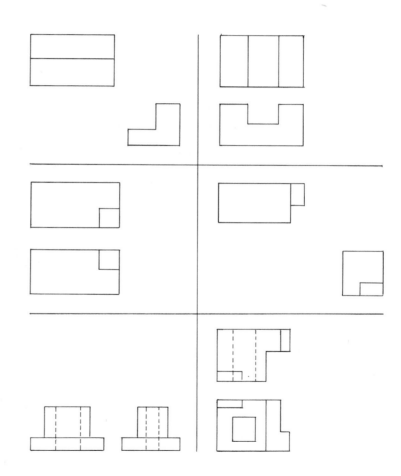

Problem 3. Pictorials

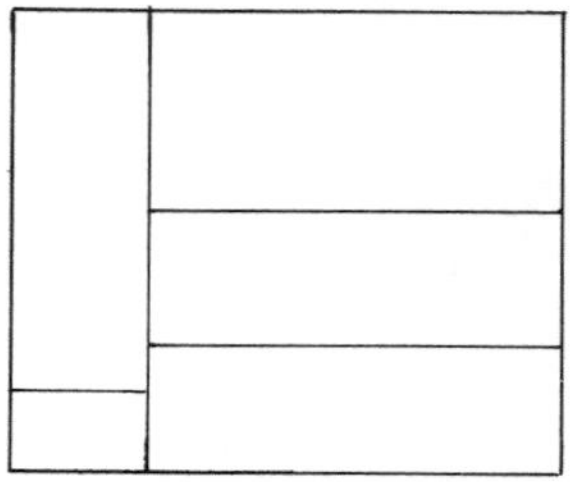

1. Make an isometric drawing of the three-step unit as seen from the front right corner.
2. Make a 1–2 cabinet drawing of the three-step unit choosing the best angle.

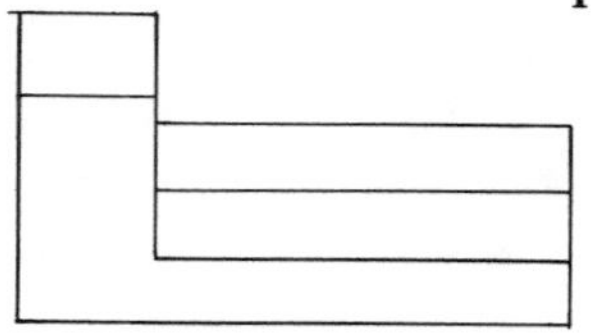

THREE-STEP UNIT

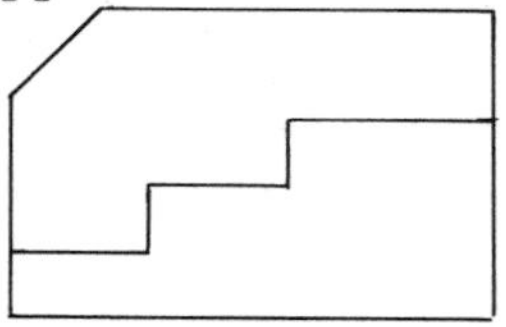

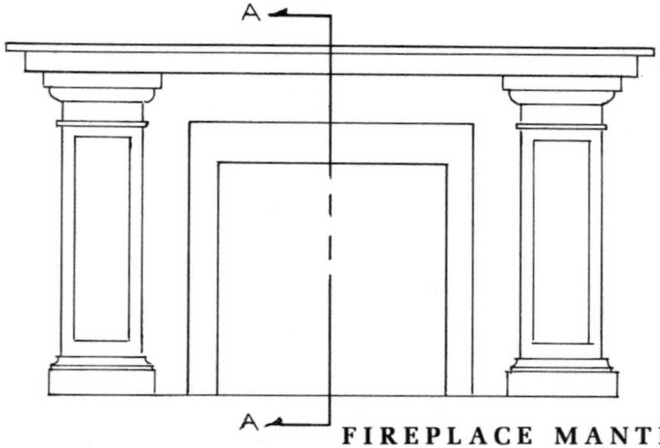

FIREPLACE MANTLE

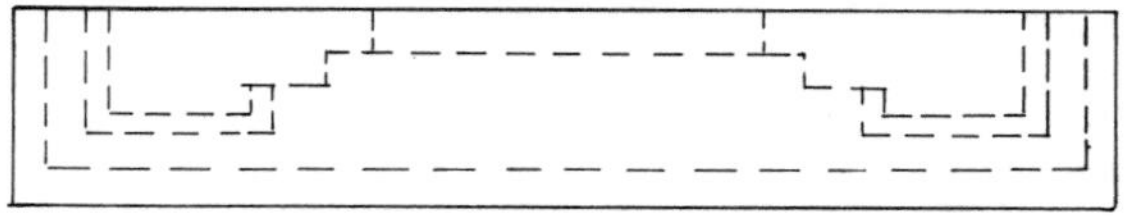

SECTIONS

1. Construct a vertical section of fireplace mantle taken at AA.
2. Construct a horizontal section choosing the best position for the cutting plane.

Problem 4. True Size and Shape

1. *Check true length views.*

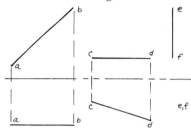

2. *Find true length of each line.*

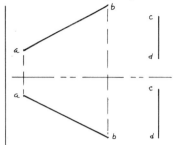

3. *Find true size and shape.*

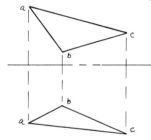

4. *Find true size and shape.*

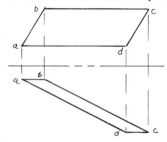

5. *Find true size and shape.*

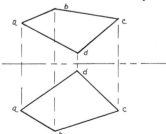

6. *Find true size and shape.*

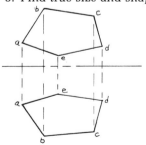

Problem 5. Developments

1. From the top and front *views of the* truncated regular hexagonal pyramid shown below, develop the pattern for the sides, top, and bottom. Use same scale as the drawing.

2. From the top and front *views of the* truncated oblique rectangular pyramid shown below, develop a pattern for the sides, top, and bottom. Use same scale as the drawing.

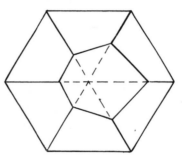

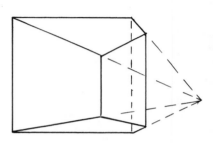

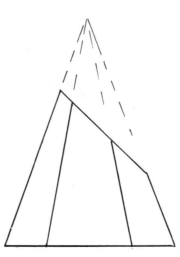

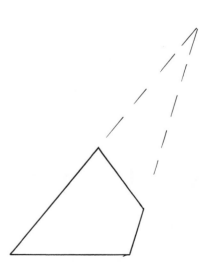

Problem 6. Developments

Find the true shape of each surface of the three-dimensional tent set piece represented below.

Use same scale as the drawing.

Problem 7. Developments

PLAN AND ELEVATION OF A SETTING WITH RAKED FLOOR AND CEILING

1. *Find true size and shape of walls and ceiling.*
2. *Assemble in model form.*

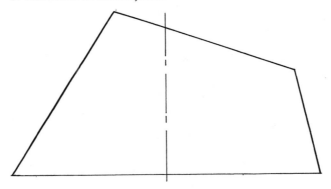

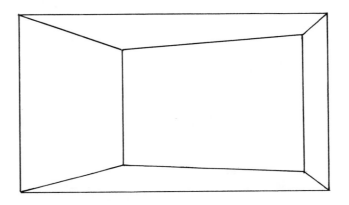

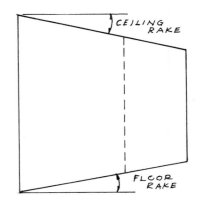

Part Three   Perspective in the Theatre

The Graphics of Perspective

A perspective drawing is the pictorial representation of a three-dimensional form in the two dimensions of the drawing paper. Although it is not a working drawing, it is a means of representing or communicating a creative form or scenic idea. For the visual artist, this is a natural skill whether it is found in a preliminary scribble or finished drawing. Others less gifted but equally inspired may want to use the graphics of perspective as an aid to formulating and presenting their visual ideas.

Perspective in the theatre is used in two forms. First, in the two-dimensional perspective found in the designer's sketch or representation of a scenic object. And secondly, as three-dimensional perspective associated with theatrical illusion or a stylistic concept.

The first, though used primarily as a stage design presentation, is also utilized in other disciplines such as architecture and interior design. The second example is purely theatrical in its origin, spectacular achievement of baroque theatre and present-day use. Since three-dimensional perspective is an outgrowth of two-dimensional perspective, it is logical to start with the latter.

16

Two-dimensional Perspective

A Basic Concept of Perspective

Perspective is described by Serlio* as an inspection or looking into by shortening of the sight. Although this is a more philosophical observation than practical analysis it does express or anticipate the initial concept of the graphics of perspective, *foreshortening*. To understand foreshortening is the first step toward being able to visualize the optics of perspective.

Signs of Spatial Perception

Foreshortening is experienced every day. Everyone has a natural perception of space. Our two eyes and their simultaneous vision are mainly responsible for the ability to judge objects in depth or in the round. This judgment, however, is dependent on several natural signs of space so familiar that they have become intuitive. We are so accustomed, for example, to seeing depth or distance in the converging horizontal lines of a railroad or fence, the gradation of a color in the sky or down a wall, the receding quality of certain colors, the reduction of size of distant objects, and the falloff of light and

*Sabastiano Serlio, *Architettura*, 1584, Second Book.

the cast of shadows. If too many of these signs are changed, our judgment is upset or fooled.

In effect, the graphics of perspective can be described as the manipulation of the optics of the eye by altering the natural signs of space perception, thereby fooling the eye and, subsequently, the observer into seeing greater depth or distance than actually is there.

Visual Foreshortening vs. Graphic Foreshortening

The signs of space perception involve normal *visual* foreshortening. To transpose visual foreshortening into *graphic* foreshortening on the drawing board, two assumptions have to be made.

Because the eye through peripheral vision is able to see more than is practical to draw, the first assumption is that all verticals are drawn perpendicular to the ground. This is true in the center of the eye's vision but not true of the extreme right and left areas. Vertical lines seem to converge or diverge depending on whether the observer is on the ground or high above. The second assumption is that the horizon line is a straight line parallel to the ground. This is not true of vi-

H L

VISUAL PERSPECTIVE
The favorite tourist photo of the Little Square, Rothenburg. Note that from each building all horizontal lines converge to a common point on the superimposed horizontal line (HL).

SIGNS OF SPATIAL PERCEPTION
Converging lines, gradation of the sky, size reduction, shadows increase our sense of depth.

sual foreshortening in which the horizon seems to curve around the observer in a gentle arc.

Cone of Vision

Added to these basic assumptions is the position of the observer in the most desirable or ideal location of the *observation point*. To capture an approximation or illusion of the visual foreshortening on paper, the best location of the observation point (OP) is at a distance from the stage or proscenium opening that provides a cone of vision not greater than 30°. In other words, the angle between lines drawn on the extreme right and left sides of the object, or arrangement of objects, to OP should approximate 30°. It is possible, of course, to set up a graphic perspective system with an OP closer to the stage or with a cone of vision greater than 30°, but the resulting graphic foreshortening is distorted or exaggerated. An extreme distortion is sometimes done for design reasons to achieve an exaggerated style and not a true foreshortened representation.

PERSPECTIVE SYSTEM

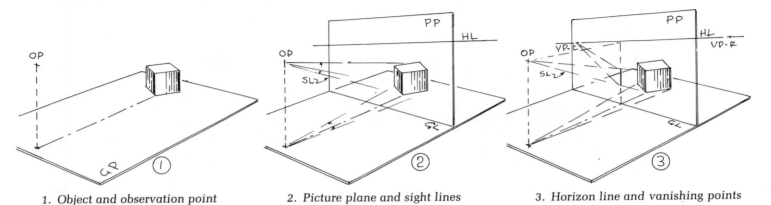

1. Object and observation point

2. Picture plane and sight lines

3. Horizon line and vanishing points

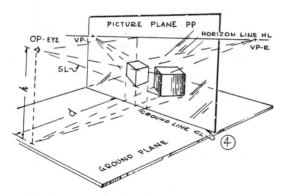

4. Transposing the object onto the
   picture plane

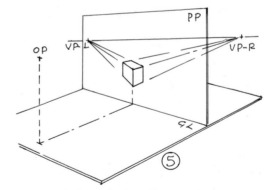

5. Two-dimensional perspective

Terminology

The *horizon line* (HL) and *observation point* (OP) are two perspective terms that will be subjected to constant reference. HL and OP are, for the most part, inseparable. The height of HL, for example, is determined by the distance OP is off the ground. *Picture plane* (PP), *ground line* (GL), *sight lines* (SL), and *vanishing point* (VP) are the remaining terms or components that need to be known to understand the graphics of foreshortening or technique of transposing an object seen in space onto the drafting board. The function of these components within a perspective system can be explained with a little visual imagination.

On page 104 is a pictorial representation of the components that make up a perspective system. The easiest plane of the system to visualize is the large horizontal plane that is parallel to, or sitting on, the ground. This is the ground plane (G) and, for theatrical use, can be the stage floor. The object (O) or stage setting is located in space by direct reference to the ground plane. The object, such as the box shown, may be hovering above or sitting on (G).

The eye or observation point (OP) is arbitrarily placed in a position to reveal the object in a favorable view or, if so desired, in a distorted view. This is normally a position a little above (G) and from a center view or from a position not too extremely right or left. The distance of OP from the object decides how lifelike the foreshortening will appear. To place OP too close, thereby creating an angle or cone of vision greater than 30°, will produce what has already been described as a distorted view.

The picture plane (PP) is an imaginary transparent plane placed between OP and the object. It is usually perpendicular to the ground and its line of intersection with the ground plane forms the *groundline* (GL). In the theatre, PP is normally considered to be at the proscenium opening or slightly upstage at the beginning of the setting.

The perspective system is almost complete except for the location of the horizon line (HL). As was mentioned earlier the height of OP off the ground determines the height of HL, which is drawn parallel to GL on the picture plane.

A close study of the perspective system soon reveals that if the eye is placed at the observation point, all sight lines emanating from it pass through the picture plane on their way to the object. It may help to imagine a sight line as a taut string drawn from the corner of the object to the eye. The point where the string touches the picture plane is the same, to the eye, as the actual point on the object. In reality, any other point or points on the same sight line register as a single point to the eye. It follows that if several sight lines are drawn from key points on the object there will be enough corresponding points on the picture plane to draw with connecting lines a representation or picture of the object as it appears in three-dimensional space.

The fact that the eye sees all points on a single sight line as one is a basic concept of graphic perspective. To visualize what has happened in space is essential to understanding the mechanics of drafting that are necessary to transpose this concept onto the drawing board.

17

The Graphics of Two-dimensional Perspective

The transposing of *visual* foreshortening into *graphic* foreshortening returns to drafting techniques. The familiar perspective components are arranged as they would appear in a top and front view with frequent reference to a side view. The basic difference is that the front view becomes a *perspective* view.

Top View

The object or arrangement of objects are, of course, the essential element in the top view. It is a scaled drawing to maintain proportions within the forthcoming perspective and appears on the ground plane or plane of the paper. The top view of the cube in this example has been altered to add interest and to also create a greater difference between the top and side views of an otherwise simple form.

   The picture plane, which in the top view will be a line, is placed in front of the object. The observation point is located slightly left of center and at a distance that will provide a cone of vision of 30° or less. The horizon line and groundline will be drawn after a check with the side view.

Side View

The side of the object in this example is used primarily for height dimensions. For that reason it is located on the groundline or on the level of the object if it is not touching the ground. Although the horizon line is drawn in the front view, it is established in the side view at a height to best reveal the object. An extremely placed HL, too high or too low, will distort the perspective as much as a wide cone of vision. The horizon line in this example is placed above the object to more clearly illustrate the vanishing points. The distance between HL and GL is the height of HL in the front view.

Front View

The front view, or perspective of the object, is developed between OP and PP. In the example the drawing appears cramped, but in a wider arrangement of objects, such as those that might appear in a stage setting, OP would be at a greater distance from PP, allowing sufficient room for the development of the perspective view.

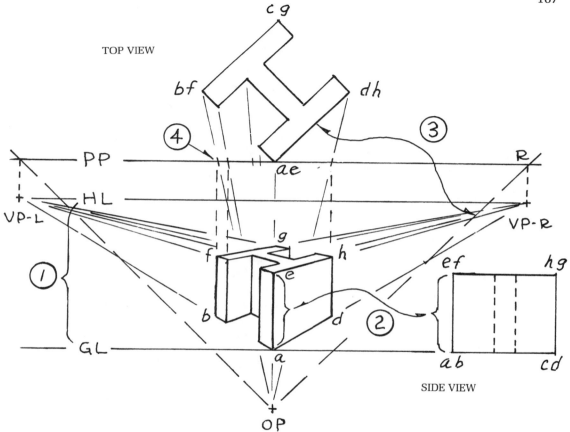

TOP VIEW

SIDE VIEW

GRAPHICS OF TWO-DIMENSIONAL PERSPECTIVE

A two vanishing-point perspective view developed below top view of the object. Side view is used for height references. 1) Location of groundline and horizon line to begin perspective view; 2) foremost edge of object touching PP; 3) location of right vanishing point (VP-R); 4) sight line intersection points on PP in top view.

Sight Lines and Vanishing Points

Because the object is placed with one edge facing OP so that none of the vertical sides are parallel to PP, each side in the perspective view will converge to a vanishing point. Since the sides are perpendicular, their vanishing points will fall on HL. To locate these points, a sight line is drawn parallel to, first, the right side (3) and then the left side of the object in top view until it meets PP. The point of intersection is dropped perpendicularly until it crosses HL, thereby locating the right vanishing point (VP-R) and the corresponding VP-L.

Perspective View

With the basic components of the perspective system in alignment, sight lines can be drawn to develop the perspective view. It is initially helpful to label principal points of the object to more easily trace the interaction of sight lines and perspective lines to the vanishing points. Although not necessary for such a simple form, the outside corners have a letter notation in both the top and side views.

The edge of the object *ae* as seen in the top view is touching PP. Therefore it can be drawn in the perspective view as an unforeshortened vertical line. It is located by dropping a vertical projection line to GL. Its height (2) is measured the same as *ea* in the side view.

Because the object is angled to PP there will be two vanishing points. To locate the right vanishing point a sight line is drawn parallel to the top view of the right side of the object (3) to intersect PP. Since parallel lines meet only in infinity, which lies in the horizon line, the point of intersection is dropped to locate the right vanishing point (VP-R) on HL. VP-L is located in the same manner.

To develop the perspective of the left side, a sight line is drawn from OP to point *bf* in the top view. Remembering that all points on a sight line appear the same to the eye, the point of intersection with PP (4) is dropped to become the vertical location of line *bf* in the perspective view. The same technique is used to locate all vertical edges of the object, to the right and left.

The foreshortened length of each vertical is established by drawing lines to the right and left vanishing points from the already established perspective vertical *ea*. Foreshortened horizontal lines are

connected and construction lines are erased to complete the perspective view.

Drop-point Perspective

Since most of the foreshortened view is developed by sight-line points on PP *dropped* into the perspective view, this method is sometimes referred to as drop-point perspective. As a graphic perspective technique, it is less confusing if one always keeps in mind that the eye sees all points on a sight line the same; that parallel lines meet on HL; and that parallel planes use the same vanishing point. These same rules apply in a much simpler way when the object or arrangement of objects is placed with surfaces parallel and/or perpendicular to the picture plane.

One Vanishing Point

Perspective with a single vanishing point is the oldest form of foreshortening, dating from Serlio to the Bibienas. It is adaptable to times when most scenery was parallel to the apron.

If an object is positioned so that its

GRAPHICS OF ONE VANISHING POINT

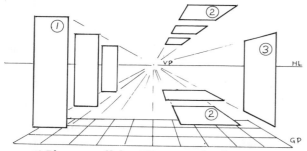

a 1) *Plane parallel to PP, perpendicular to GP;*
2) *planes parallel to GP, perpendicular to PP;*
3) *perpendicular to both GL and PP.*

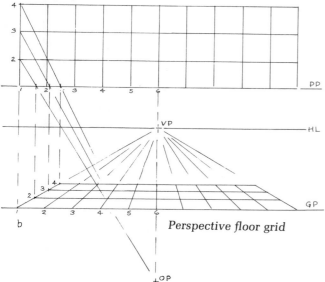

b   *Perspective floor grid*

principal surfaces are parallel and/or perpendicular to the picture plane, all its surfaces are foreshortened by converging lines to a single vanishing point located on HL directly above OP. How these planes appear in space is illustrated on page 109 (*a*). Surface (1) is parallel to PP and perpendicular to the ground plane (GP); (2) is parallel to GP, perpendicular to PP; (3) is perpendicular to both PP and GP.

The most important surface shown is the horizontal ground plane, which has been given dimensionality as a reference plane (such as the stage floor) by dividing its surface into a grid of squares. Note that surfaces parallel to PP (1) are foreshortened in size, while surfaces perpendicular to PP (2 and 3) are foreshortened in shape as well as size.

The second part of the drawing (*b*) diagrams the method of developing the floor grid (GP) in perspective. Because all vertical lines in the top view of GP are perpendicular to PP their foreshortened counterparts in the perspective view (below) converge from measured points on PP to a single vanishing point on HL. The horizontal lines, on the other hand, are foreshortened in length and distance apart.

The horizontal lines are located in the

perspective view by sight-line projections from OP. For clarity, each line is numbered 1 through 4. Because line 1 falls on PP there is no change in dimension. The point where the sight line to horizontal line 2 crosses PP is dropped to intersect the perspective position of vertical line 1, thereby establishing the foreshortened horizontal line 2. Horizontal lines 3 and 4 are located by the same technique to complete the perspective floor grid.

Proportional Subdividing

Drawings on this page demonstrate a method of quickly subdividing horizontal dimensions into perspective of either the two-dimensional perspective of a scenic form or the arbitrarily foreshortening of an element of scenery. 1) Plan of a form with regularly spaced openings. 2) Perspective view without openings. Along a temporary base line (BL), points mark the true dimension of each opening numbered 1 through 7. A line is produced from 7 through the lower corner of the form to intersect HL, establishing a vanishing point for the rest of the point on BL. Where each line crosses the bottom edge of the perspective, form will subdivide it

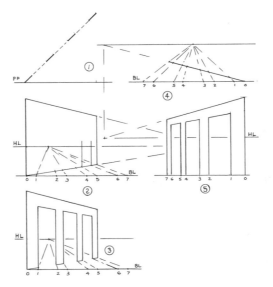

into graduated perspective. 3) Verticals and deaders are added; BL and construction lines are erased to complete the drawing. 4) An arbitrary setup to foreshorten and angled scenic form. True base dimensions are projected onto plan. 5) Finished elevation incorporating foreshortened dimensions.

Perspective of Circles, Arched Opening, and Details

a. Circle in perspective is plotted on two diagonals, horizontal and vertical center lines, within the perspective view of the square circumscribing the circle. It is drawn freehand through points tangent to the sides and perpendicular to diagonals.

b. Semicircular arch is parallel to PP. Center of curvature is plotted in perspective. First circle is unforeshortened. Second circle is regular but reduced in radius.

c. Irregular arch is plotted on a perspective grid.

d. Decorative detail is plotted on a perspective grid.

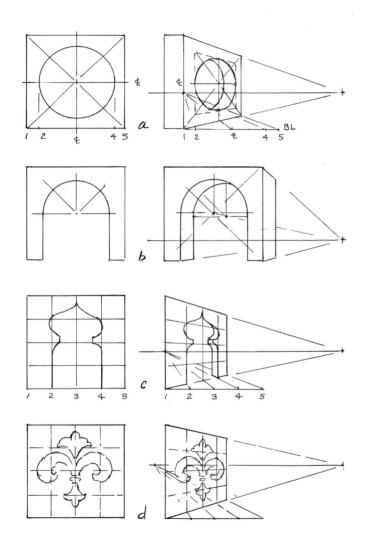

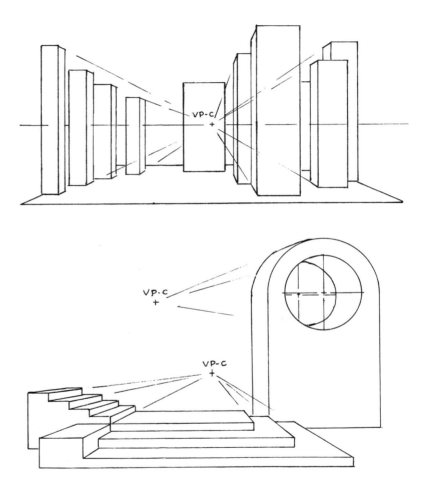

PERSPECTIVE EXAMPLE: ONE VANISHING POINT
The second plane of the circle is not distorted but is foreshortened as the center is shifted in perspective.

18

Perspective Floor Grid and Designer's Sketch

The designer's sketch has two basic functions. First, it is the primary means of thinking and creating three-dimensional scenic forms in two dimensions before going into the three-dimensionality of a scaled model. Second, as a finished drawing, the sketch is a convenient and informative method of communicating a scenographic concept or dramatic moment in the theatre. With this mind, the young designer is interested in being able to present his or her ideas as accurately as possible in sketch form.

Use of Perspective Grid

Some designers who are accomplished visual artists do not rely on the graphics of perspective. Their natural skill and sense of scale provide a personal technique or way of thinking and creating. For the developing designer, however, the perspective grid is one method of thinking and working with the three-dimensional forms in space, yet within the two dimensions of the drawing paper.

The many odd angles found in the floor plan of the average stage setting do not lend themselves to the mechanics of formal drop-point perspective with an observation point and numerous vanishing points. The perspective grid method, although an approximation, is simple and accurate enough for a design presentation.

The advantages of using a perspective floor grid for a two-dimensional perspective drawing are fourfold. 1) After the initial usage of the observation point to construct the perspective grid, it is no longer needed to complete the perspective view. 2) A perspective floor grid can be developed for a specific audience-stage relationship to be saved for reuse, over and over. 3) The perspective can be drawn at a reduced scale to save drafting space and then proportionally enlarged to a desirable sketch size. 4) Finally, a designer's sketch started in this manner provides a framework for calculating the three-dimensional perspective of foreshortened scenery for either a scenic illusion or a design concept.

The Floor Plan

The basic steps for the use of the perspective grid are illustrated on page 113. The development of a perspective sketch of a simple unit of scenery begins with its floor plan (a), which is located on the stage by means of a scaled grid. The grid of 2′ squares are numbered for clarity. A

PERSPECTIVE FLOOR PLAN
AND THE DESIGNER'S SKETCH

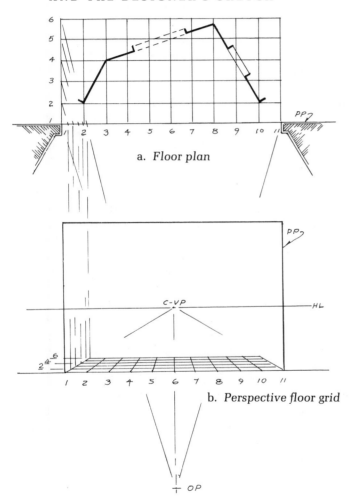

a. Floor plan

b. Perspective floor grid

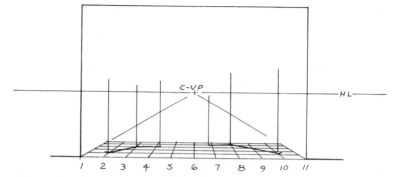

c. Floor plan in perspective

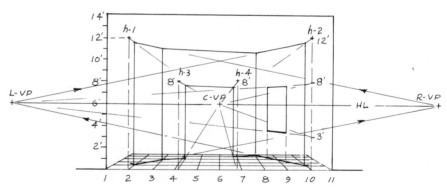

d. Vanishing points located; measuring poles h-1 and h-2 determine wall heights, h-3 and h-4 door height.

perspective of the same grid (b) is placed directly below. The proscenium opening, which is also the picture plane, frames the downstage edge. The perspective grid has been developed with OP at a distance to provide a flattering cone of vision (30°). The horizon line in this example is fixed at 6'. The vertical edges of PP are marked at 1' intervals at the same scale as the floor grid. The next step (c) is to draw the floor plan in perspective by cross-reference, square by square, with the original plan (a). Vertical lines are drawn at each corner to a yet-to-be-determined height.

Measuring Poles

It is important to remember at this juncture that all true heights and widths lie in the picture plane. This information is transferred into the perspective view by the use of temporary measuring poles for heights and additional perspective lines to the central vanishing point (C-VP) parallel to the floor grid. A measuring pole can be established anywhere within PP on a regular perspective line in the grid or on a temporary parallel line. The height in perspective is located on a line drawn from the measured height in PP to C-VP.

In the illustration, for example, h-1 in (d) is a 12' pole raised on vertical line 2 in the floor grid. The true height at the top of the pole is projected back to C-VP until it intersects the downstage edge of the stage-right flat. Pole h-2 on vertical line 10 performs the same function to find the height of the downstage-left edge. Additional vanishing points will be needed to find the height of the upstage edges.

Finding and Using Additional Vanishing Points

Since the walls of the scenic unit sit askew to all lines in the floor grid, it will be necessary to find their individual vanishing points. The vanishing points for the stage-right-and-left walls are located, without using OP, by producing their bottom edges in the floor plan to intersect HL. The stage-right base line, for example, is extended to establish the right vanishing point (R-VP) on HL. Its top is drawn in perspective by a line from the new R-VP to the downstage edge of the right wall. Where the line crosses the upstage vertical edge completes the perspective view of the right wall. The vanishing point of the left wall (L-VP) and top edge are found by the same process.

Because the rake of the back wall is so flat, its vanishing point will fall off the paper. It is drawn in perspective by connecting the top and bottom to the left and right walls. The sides of the door opening are projected upward from the plan. Their respective heights are determined by creating two new measuring poles, h-3 and h-4, by drawing a line from C-VP, through the door opening in the plan to the picture plane. The 8' height on each pole is projected back to C-VP. Where they cross the door jambs marks the height of the door in perspective.

The window, like the door, is spotted in the floor plan. Verticals are raised to an undetermined height. Using the measuring pole of the stage-left wall, the window sill (3'0") and the header (8'0") are transferred to the downstage edge by using lines to C-VP. The vanishing point of the left wall is used to locate in perspective the heights of the header and sill.

The basic form is now represented in two-dimensional perspective. Wall thicknesses and details can be added including a figure to give the drawing scale (d). Because the horizon line in this example is 6' above the stage floor, it becomes an easy reference line for placing an actor in the scene. The head of the average figure would be close to touching HL anywhere in the setting.

e. Finished perspective sketch

Sketch Examples

To demonstrate the use of the perspective grid as an aid to preparing a sketch of a set design three diverse examples are presented on the following pages. The first shows the steps taken to develop a sketch for a convention interior setting placed behind the frame of a proscenium type theatre.

The second example is a hypothetical production bringing together several theatrical staging devices. A ramped stage floor thrusting through the proscenium opening is countered by a sloping ceiling.

This type of open staging places elements of scenery ahead of the proscenium as well as the picture plane of the perspective setup. The cone of vision is held to the proscenium open allowing the sides to flare spread slightly.

The last is an imagined scene in a thrust stage theatre. The angled and elevated viewpoint in the sketch is a variation of the perspective grid method with two vanishing points. The angle is optional and can be reversed if the designer wants to show a view of the setting from the opposite direction.

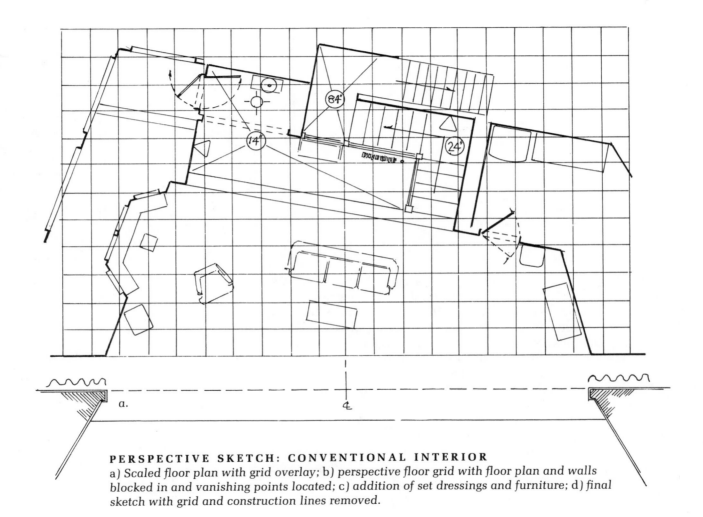

a.

c.

PERSPECTIVE SKETCH: CONVENTIONAL INTERIOR
a) Scaled floor plan with grid overlay; b) perspective floor grid with floor plan and walls
blocked in and vanishing points located; c) addition of set dressings and furniture; d) final
sketch with grid and construction lines removed.

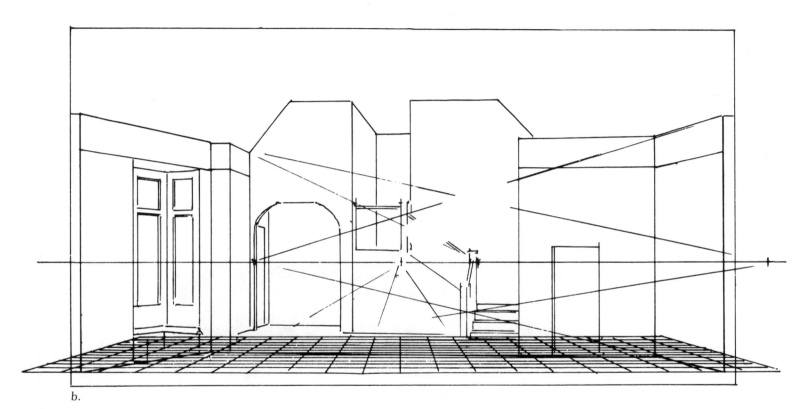

b.

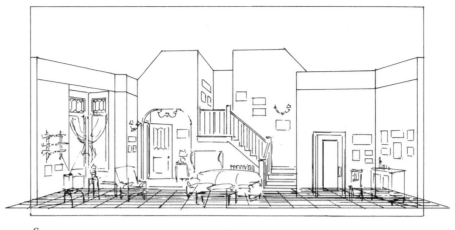

c.

d.

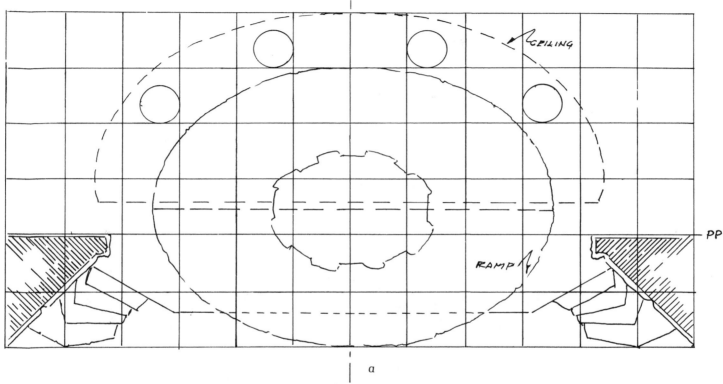

a

PERSPECTIVE SKETCH: SLOPING FLOOR AND CEILING

a) *Floor plan with grid overlay: note position of PP with scenery ahead of proscenium. b) Split view showing on stage-left side the perspective grid and the method of determining the ramp of the floor in perspective: 1) perspective grid; 2) a second perspective grid overhead to locate slope of the ceiling; 3) position of PP as it cuts ramped floor and sloped ceiling; 4) center line; c) finished sketch. It should be noted in this example that the grid has been expanded to 3' squares. Some designers prefer a rectangular grid 2' across and 3' deep (upstage) that looks nearer square in perspective.*

b

c

PERSPECTIVE SKETCH: THE THRUST STAGE

An angled and elevated view of a scene on the thrust stage. The perspective grid can be reversed for variety. a) Floor plan with grid overlay; b) perspective grid; c) final sketch.

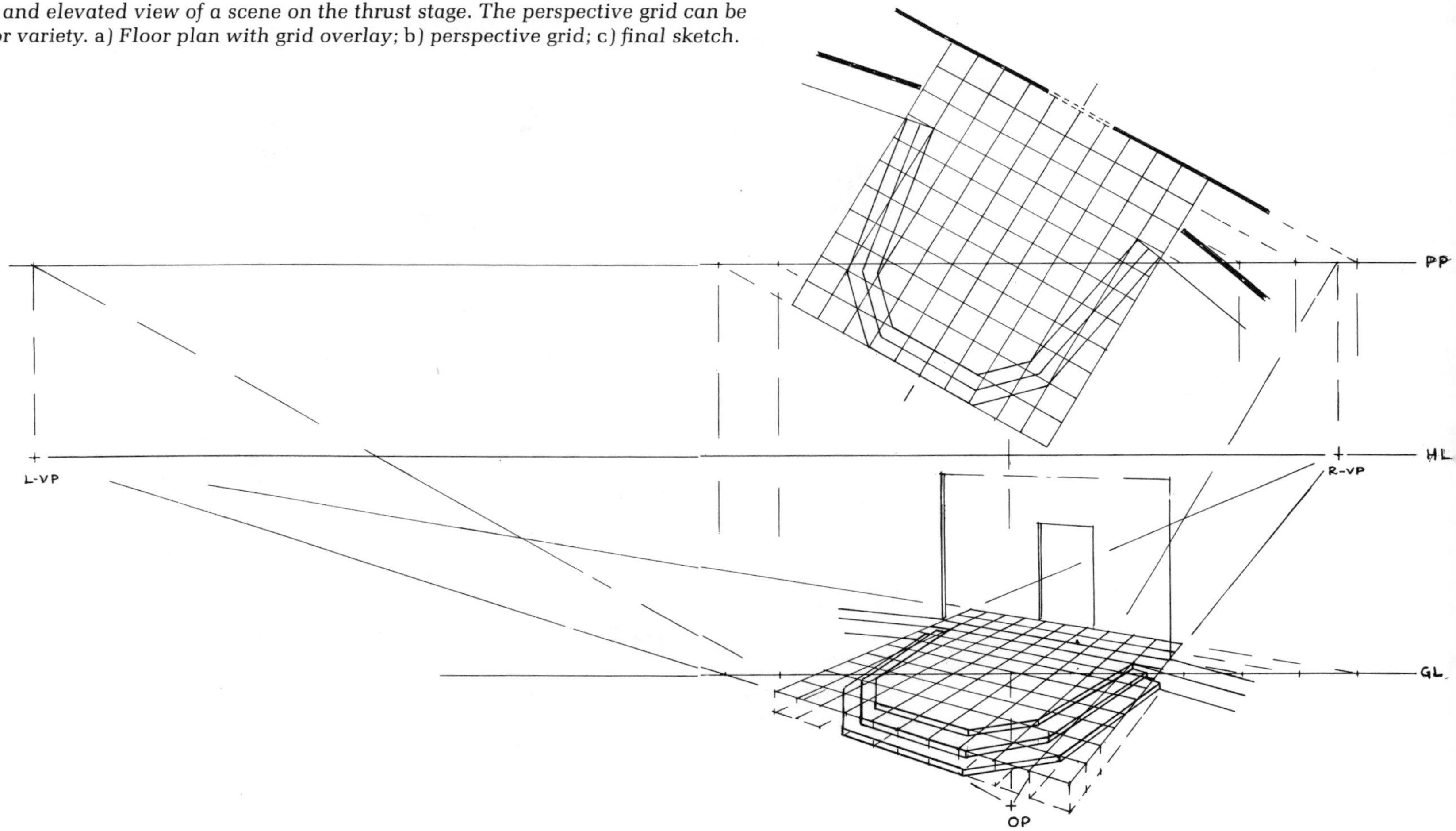

PP

HL

L-VP

R-VP

GL

OP

19

Three-dimensional Perspective

Three-dimensional perspective is the physical foreshortening of an object to give the illusion of greater size or distance. When, for example, an element of scenery is foreshortened it is actually built and painted in perspective to create the illusion of greater space than the volume of the stage. For many centuries the graphics of three-dimensional perspective has fascinated artists in the theatre more as a means of achieving a spectacular illusion than as a dramatic tool.

Theatrical Perspective

A brief review of the origin of perspective soon reveals that the theatre was the cradle, experimental laboratory, showcase, and last resting place of many flamboyant uses of perspective. It is safe to assume, without too much fear of contradiction, that the earliest uses of three-dimensional perspective in an organized manner first appeared in the *theatre*.

We know, for example, that the study of the science of perspective began in Renaissance times and that many Renaissance artists and architects also designed for the theatre. We also know that these same artists were attracted to the writings of Vitruvius, the ancient Roman who, rather freely, interpreted the form and substance of Greek classical art, architecture, and theatre. Perspective and scenery painting appear as virtually synonymous terms in Vitruvius' use of the word "scenographia" to describe the already lost formula of perspective in Greek times.

Such familiar Italian names as Alberti, Peruzzi, Serlio, and Vignola and, later, Palladio, Scamozzi, Pozzi, Juvara, and the Bibienas are associated with the development and use of perspective in the theatre as well as being leaders in the art and architecture of the Renaissance and baroque periods.

In the middle of the sixteenth century one of the first theatrical applications of perspective appears in Sabastiano Serlio's formalized stage settings and amphitheatres. Serlio, like many other Renaissance artists, experimented with perspective in an attempt to bring greater reality to a flat surface. They all strove to break through the two-dimensional canvas to create the illusion of a more lifelike three-dimensional world. Though Serlio's experiments are about a century after Leone Battista Alberti's first treatise on perspective in 1435, he followed the direction of his contemporary teacher, Baldassarre Pe-

124

ruzzi in expressing a more dimensional
and less geometric approach to the use of
perspective in the theatre.

While the perspective of Serlio's settings (pp. 124—25) is not completely il-
lusory to modern eyes, it does envolve
the foreshortening of three-dimensional
forms to create a feeling of greater distance than is actually on the stage. The
wide cone of vision or close positioning
of the single central vanishing point flat-
tens the forms into what might be described as an oversized sculptural relief.

In the latter portion of the sixteenth
century, Andrea Palladio followed the ra-
tional of Serlio with a more permanent
theatre structure in Vicenza. The perspective vistas in the Teatro Olympico, which
were actually planned by Vincenzo Scamozzi after Palladio's death, are more
naturalistic than Serlio's street scenes and
more ambitious in the number of views.
Although the view of each vista is at a
different angle, the perspective system
within each opening is the same as Serlio's with the exception of the use of a
smaller cone of vision. The perspective,
as a result, is more convincing. The front
of the houses (the side facing the audi-
ence) is treated without perspective, in
the Serlian manner, reducing in scale as

Scena Comica.

a SEBASTIANO SERLIO

THEATRICAL PERSPECTIVE

a) *A comedy scene by Sabastiano Serlio, 1545. A single central vanishing point perspective of a street scene—an early stylistic use of perspective in the theatre. b) Plan and section showing the three-dimensionality of the perspective. Note the closeness of the vanishing point (VP). Courtesy of Beinecke Rare Book and Manuscript Library, Yale University.*

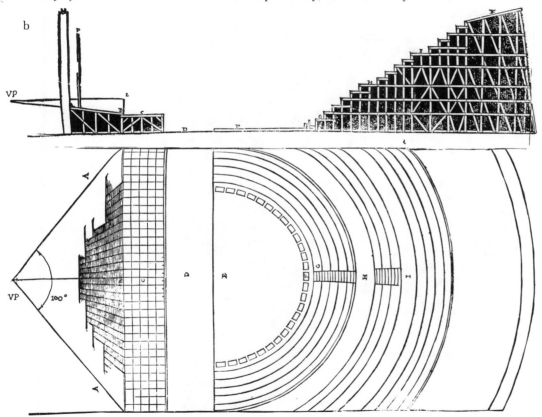

TEATRO OLIMPICO, VICENZA

a

Andrea Palladio's permanent theatre with three-perspective vista by Scamozzi: a) view of the stage and a portion of the elliptical seating; b) closeup of the larger central opening with its perspective vista. The floor and the buildings converge to a single vanishing point.

b

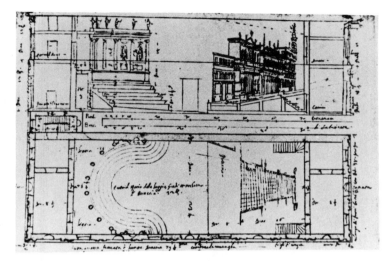

TEATRO OLIMPICO, SABBIONETA

An intimate theatre by Vincenzo Scamozzi with a large single perspective vista: a) plan and section (Courtesy Rockefeller Theatrical Print Collection, Yale University); b) sketch from photograph of reconstruction. Marks on the painted landscape on the stage walls indicate that the beamed roof may have been covered with a sky-painted ceiling.

the eye moves upstage. The knotty problem of locating the vanishing point of angled walls on a slanted floor remain to be solved later.

The single vista of Teatro Olimpico at Sabbioneta, also by Scamozzi, is a more successful illusion, but like Serlio and the theatre in Vicenza, the perspective is ornamental. The dramatic action is to take place in front of, and not within, the vista. It is a part of the paradox of the early use of perspective in the theatre. The contradiction of a very real background for an abstract place reflects Roman and Greek classical theatre, yet it is a movement toward a stage setting.

As the theatre grew away from the stationary scene and scenery began to be movable, the need arose for greater variety and excitement than the static qualities of one-point perspective could provide. The angling of building within the scene and the locating of vanishing points for each side resulted in a two-point perspective technique that was exploited to the fullest in the flat planes of the wing and backdrop style of scenery. Eventually the desire for a grander scale and a more dynamic expression of the designer's fantasies lead to the angling of scenery itself.

Not until late in the seventeenth century is there a recorded method for solving

128

the foreshortening of three-dimensional perspective. Andrea Pozzo in his work *Prospettiva Dei Pettroi E Architti* sets forth in two volumes of diagrammatic illustrations and profuse explanations several methods for figuring the perspective of elaborate wing and backdrop settings. Pozzo gives an insight into the working techniques of such baroque designers as Juvarra, Piranesi, and the Bibiena family. Pozzo's procedure for foreshortening a room or vesta into a series of flat or angled wings dominates the scene with only slight deviations to the end of the eighteenth century (p. 128).

In the nineteenth century, the more frequent use of diagonal scenery and the appearance of the *box set* on the sloped stage floor posed new problems for the stage designer. Paulo Landriani, in 1815, presented a method that more or less adopted the Pozzo foreshortening procedure to the box set or nonwing and backdrop setting (p. 130). Later in the century, Jules De LaGournerie, in his *Traite De Perspective*, devotes a section at the end of the book to theatre perspective. His method is a more integrated and unique use of seventeenth-century foreshortening procedures applied to the box set (pp. 132–33) and is adaptable to present-day theatre as will be shown.

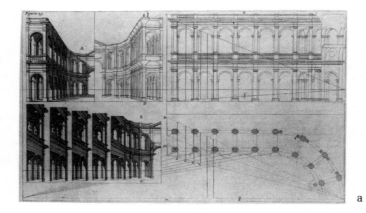

a

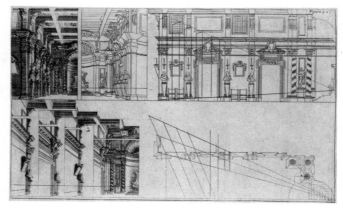

b

ANDERA POZZO'S PERSPECTIVE DIAGRAMS

a) *Half plan and side view demonstrating method of foreshortening an arcade into wing and back drop setting; b) foreshortening a room onto a slanted wing arrangement. (See further explanation, p.131.) Courtesy Beinecke Rare Book and Manuscript Library, Yale University.*

BAROQUE THEATRE PERSPECTIVE
A carefully constructed model of a Giuseppe Galli Bibiena setting. A fanciful and theatrical assemblage of architecture featuring several vanishing points breaking the monotonous composition of the central single vanishing point.

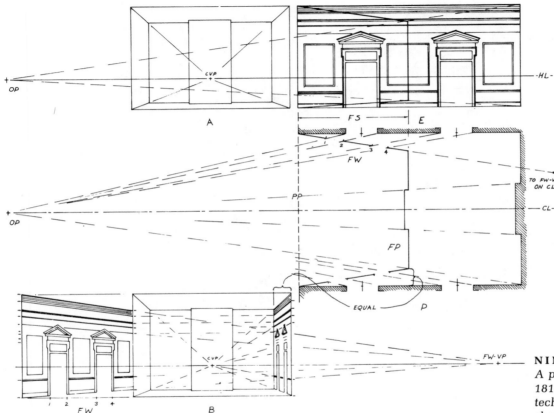

NINETEENTH-CENTURY PERSPECTIVE
A perspective system by Paulo Landriani,
1815, adapting Renaissance foreshortening
techniques to a box setting. A) Front elevation
showing basic forms of foreshortened room:
E) elevation of full-scale room, side view;
FS) overlay of foreshortened section; FW)
foreshortened side wall in plan. B) Layout
of foreshortened wall (FW) with its vanishing
point.

By the end of the century and in the early nineteen hundreds the use and knowledge of theatrical perspective were predominately in the hands of the scene painter, as the artist/architect had all but left the theatre. Being closest in time to our present-day theatre, it unfortunately makes the greatest impression. To many the mention of perspective in the theatre evoked a rememberance of the lurid examples at the beginning of the twentieth century. Perspective in the hands of the scene painter was primarily two-dimensional, painted perspective in the best tradition of romantic realism.

Theatrical Perspective Today

Perspective as an illusion enjoys only limited use in present-day theatre, partly owning to the modern concept of scene design and partly because of the less favorable stage and auditorium relationship. Gone are the sloped stage floor and the horseshoe-shaped house with its "perspective eye" in the carefully placed ducal box of the theatre that one time was the home of the perspective *tour de force* of the eighteenth century. In addition, the popular new theatre forms such as thrust

and arena stages do not lend themselves to a perspective illusion.

On the other hand, there are many times the designer has to create a feeling of more space than actually exists on the stage. Graphic perspective may be sharpened to intensify the composition or exaggerated beyond belief into a design concept. There are also those occasions when a designer is asked to re-create the perspective of historical theatre in either serious retrospect or as a gentle spoof.

In any event, the first steps in learning the graphics of three-dimensional perspective are to be able to locate vanishing points in space and to develop a foreshortened shape. It will be noted in the historical examples that that was accomplished with cross information from an aligned plan or top view and side view.

Top and Side View Method

The oldest method of solving the graphics of three-dimensional perspective in the theatre may be called, for want of a better name, the top and side view method. It takes its name from the unique use of the two views for solving three-dimensional foreshortening as well as the develop-

ment of normal two-dimensional perspective. We have already seen examples of its sophisticated use by Pozzo, Landriani, and LaGournerie. Essentially the system involves the alignment of the top view and side view of the object with an observation point in such a way as to collect information by cross-reference to plot a perspective view.

The drawing board setup for the top and side view method and the development of the perspective view is basically the same as an orthographic projection with minor changes. The drawing on page 135 shows the alignment of the views and the development of the perspective, which is plotted without the use of vanishing points. The object, a boxlike form, is placed at an angle so that one edge touches the picture plane. Its placement and relationship to PP are shown in the *top view*.

The alignment of the *side view* and the *top view* is different in that the side view has been placed on its side, so to speak, which makes it easier, later on, to figure the foreshortening of more complicated pieces of scenery. Both views can be rotated to place the side view into a horizontal position with the same results.

The observation point appears in both views. The distance between OP and the

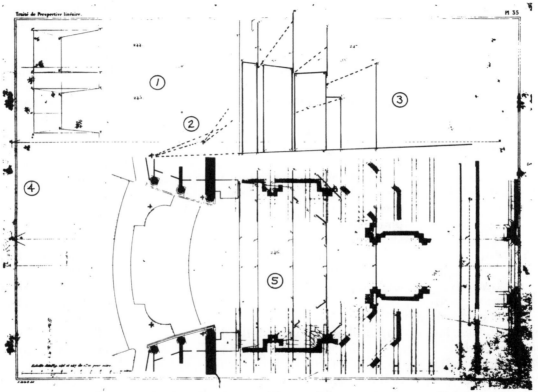

A later adaptation by Jules De LaGournerie of the Landriani system to a combination wing and box setting—plan and side view. Shaded double lines show plan of full room; single lightweight lines are the side walls and wings of the foreshortened plan: 1) schematic of plan and side view arrangement; 2) vertical sight lines to check masking of foreshortened scenery; 3) side view of foreshortened scenery elements; 4) observation point, note that it is off-center; 5) plan.

De LaGournerie adaptation—overleaf: 1) elevation of the three arches and border that make up the back wall of the foreshortened set; 2) reflected foreshortened plan; 3) counterperspective on side wall because it is angled; 4) method of bringing vertical proportions of architectural details to the plane of the border and angled side wall.

PAINTED PERSPECTIVE
Sketches from a scenic artist's notebook,
1895.

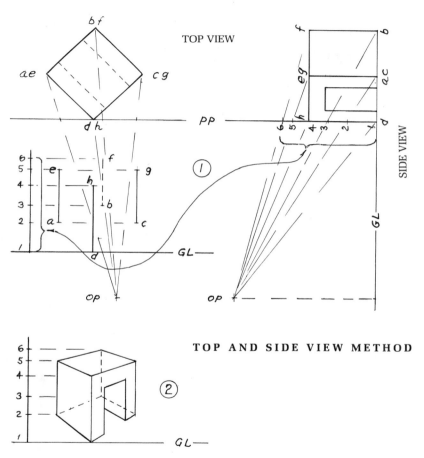

TOP VIEW

PP

SIDE VIEW

GL

OP

OP

TOP AND SIDE VIEW METHOD

GL

Top and side view of object are aligned so information from both views can be used to plot the perspective view without the use of vanishing points. 1) Points of intersection of sight lines with vertical picture plane in side view are transposed to top view. 2) Plotted perspective.

object is located in the top view, while its height off the ground is shown in the side view.

The picture plane appears as a line in both views. The intersection of PP with the ground plane (GP) in the side view marks the groundline (GL). To begin the perspective in the top view, GL is arbitrarily placed between PP and OP allowing space to develop the drawing. The groundline becomes a reference line to measure heights taken from GL in the side view.

Before the sight lines are drawn it is good practice to label the important corners of the object in each view with corresponding letters. Vertical sight lines will appear in the side view, while the horizontal sight lines are visible in the top view. Because of the regularity of the object and its position, some sight lines will overlap within and between the views.

Where the sight lines cross PP in either view designates the perspective points in the picture plane. They can be located by reference to their height off GL in the side view (1, 2, 3, 4, 5, 6) and by direct alignment under the top view. For example, the right edge of the object (e, g) is located by, first, drawing a vertical line directly under the point of intersection on

PP of the sight line to *e, g* in the top view. Next, the foreshortened length of the edge and its distance off GL (1, 2, 3) are transposed from the corresponding sight line points of intersection on PP in the side view. The length and location of all edges are found in the same manner except, of course, edge *b, h*, which lies in the picture plane and therefore is not foreshortened.

Foreshortening Solutions

The top and side view method is obviously a cumbersome method to figure two-dimensional perspectives unless the observation point is in an extreme position such as a bird's-eye view (p. 145). It is, however, the prime method for solving foreshortening. On pages 136 and 137 are two examples of foreshortening techniques in the manner of baroque theatre that have been applied to finding the perspective on the traditional wing. In the first, the wing is parallel to the apron. The top view is a horizontal half plan showing the position of the wing (1) in relation to the bays of freestanding columns. The points of intersecting sight lines in the plan are transposed to the front view (3) where in conjunction with vertical

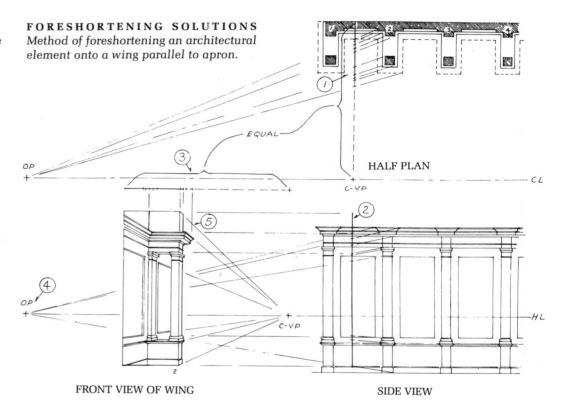

FORESHORTENING SOLUTIONS
Method of foreshortening an architectural element onto a wing parallel to apron.

HALF PLAN

FRONT VIEW OF WING   SIDE VIEW

FORESHORTENING SOLUTIONS

*Method of foreshortening
an architectural bay
onto angled wing.*

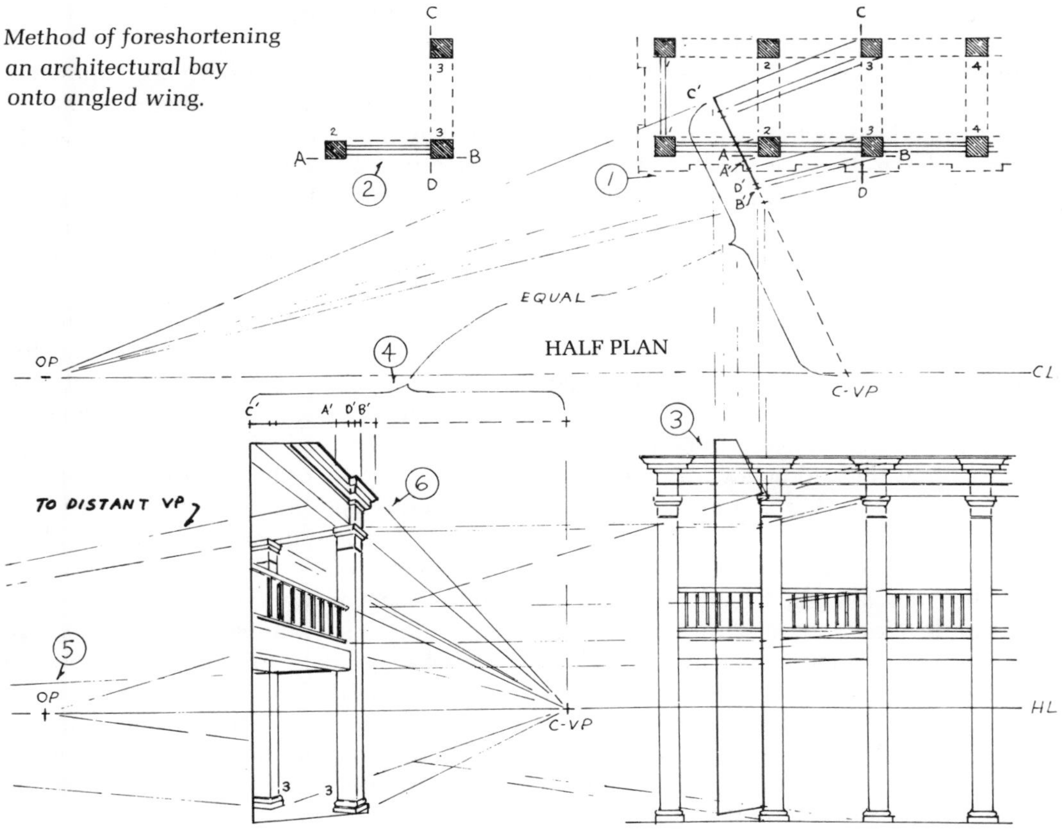

C

② D

A— —B

①

C

HALF PLAN

EQUAL

OP

④

C-VP

CL

C' A' D' B'

TO DISTANT VP

⑥

⑤

OP

C-VP

③

HL

FRONT VIEW OF WING

SIDE VIEW

sight lines, a foreshortened view of the
original architecture is constructed (5).

The second example involves a slanted
wing and more complicated architecture,
a bay with a connecting surface perpendicular to the apron (2). The procedure is
the same with the exception of the front
view, which has a second distant vanishing point falling off the paper.

20

Three-dimensional Foreshortening

Solving the foreshortening of an assembled three-dimensional object or box set is an occasional problem. The nineteenth-century techniques of Paulo Landriani (p. 130) are a good example of the use of a top and side view to develop the fore-shortened elevations of a box setting. Dimensions from the new smaller plan are transposed into the elevation of the fore-shortened wall and its new vanishing point, FW-VP.

The same technique is applied to a contemporary problem. A small assembled unit of scenery, such as a bus stop shelter (p. 139) is foreshortened to occupy less space on the stage. Again, the alignment of a top view and side view provides the means to put together a front view (3). It is *not* a perspective view, contrary to what its location between the top view and OP might suggest. The disassembled view or development is achieved with dimensions and spacing present in the various views.

Although OP is on the center line of the object in this example, it can be set up to the right or left depending on the position of the object on the stage.

Foreshortening from the Sketch and Plan

All the examples that have been shown dealt with the foreshortening of actual size whether it be a room or unit of architecture. The designer frequently uses perspective in the opposite procedure. It may begin in the sketch. The perspective is sharpened in an effort to get a greater sense of space or scale into the design. If the sketch has been developed by the perspective floor grid technique it is easy to use information from the sketch and plan to find the true shape of foreshortened scenic elements.

The example of foreshortened scenery shown on page 140 is a simple exterior setting. The first drawing shows the plan and sketch relationship. Note that there are two sets of vanishing points for each plane of the set numbered 1 through 4. B-VP is the normal vanishing point for each unit and T-VP is the foreshortened VP of the tops. All foreshortening takes place above the horizon line and none below. If HL is established at six feet or higher the foreshortening is above the actor and the stage floor remains flat.

The amount of foreshortening is decided by the designer in the sketch. The

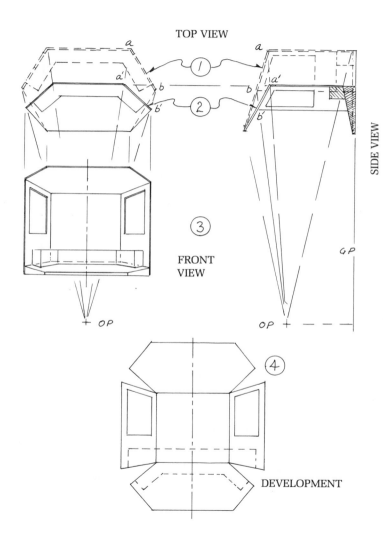

TOP VIEW

① ②

SIDE VIEW

③

FRONT
VIEW

GP

+ OP

OP +

④

DEVELOPMENT

new vanishing points (T-VP) are projected upward into the plan to a point
on the extension of the respective plane
of each house.

In the second drawing (p. 141) the foreshortened elevation is constructed by
using base-line dimensions from the plan
to locate the new vanishing point (t-VP).

**THREE-DIMENSIONAL
FORESHORTENING**
*Use of the top and side view to find the
foreshortened shape of an assembled unit of
scenery: 1) full-sized unit in top view and
side view; 2) foreshortened position in top
view and side view; 3) foreshortened front
view; 4) true size and shape of each piece in
the unit.*

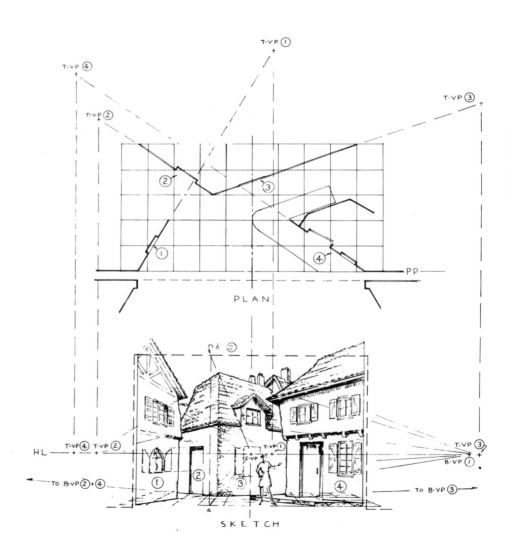

FORESHORTENING FROM SKETCH AND PLAN

Plan: walls are numbered 1 through 4.
Sketch: bottom vanishing lines to B-VP are unforeshortened or normal perspective; top vanishing point (T-VP) represents increased perspective above HL. Each top vanishing point is projected upward to intersect the extended wall in the plan.

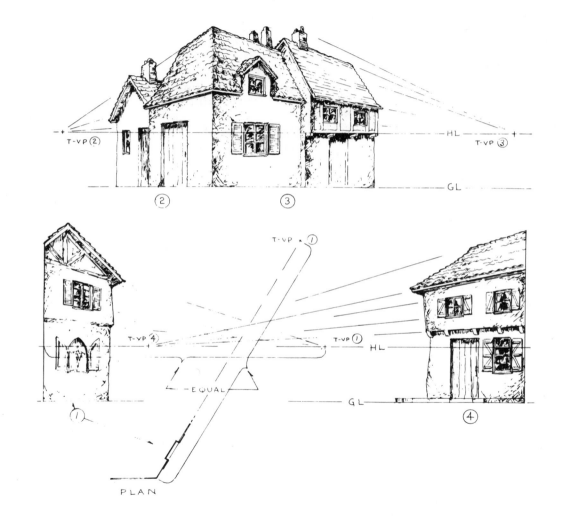

HL

T-VP ②   T-VP ③

GL

②   ③

T-VP · ①

T-VP ④   T-VP ①   HL

EQUAL

GL

①   ④

PLAN

**FORESHORTENING FROM
SKETCH AND PLAN**
*Elevation of each wall unit with
foreshortening of top: 1) location of top
vanishing point, T-VP (1) on horizon line
from equal distance in plan.*

21

Extreme
Viewpoints

Three-point Perspective

On the following pages are examples of perspective from unusual viewpoints. When the observation point is too close, too high, or too low, the original assumption that all verticals are perpendicular to the ground is no longer valid. We know that when we stand at the base of a tall building and look up, the vertical lines seem to converge. The opposite effect is experienced when looking down from a window of an upper floor. The verticals are converging to a third vanishing point above or below the horizon line.

Slanted Picture Plane

A graphic explanation of three-point perspective entails the use of a slanted picture plane. A professional photographer corrects converging vertical lines by using a swing front or PC lens (perspective correction). The lens tilts forward until parallel with the object, thereby correcting the image that falls on the negative. This is essentially what the graphics of perspective does to keep vertical lines perpendicular. It follows that if we want to find the convergence of a given situation,

we tilt the picture frame forward to an angle approximately perpendicular to the center line of the cone of vision. If the situation is reversed, a high angle of vision, the picture plane is tilted back.

The slanted picture plane serves as an explanation of three-point perspective; however, the designer should feel free to vary the angle for design reasons. Many times a vertical, or third vanishing point, can be arbitrarily established in relation to right and left vanishing points to create an object or group of objects with a convergence that is right for the composition.

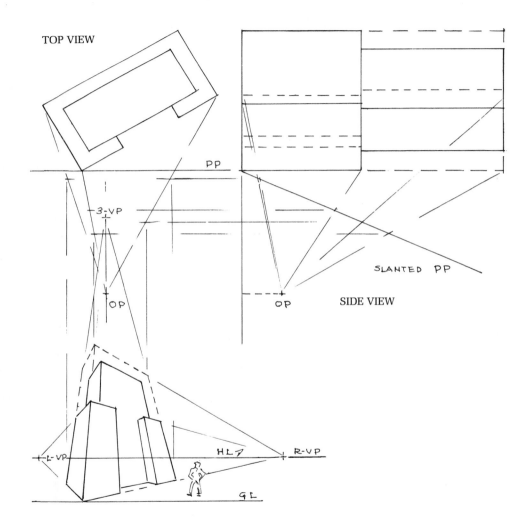

TOP VIEW

PP

3-VP

OP

SLANTED PP

OP

SIDE VIEW

HL

L-VP

R-VP

GL

SLANTED PICTURE PLANE

Low and close observation point. Object is angled to picture plane. The convergence of outside edges (dotted lines) is established in perspective by plotting. Form is extended to locate three vanishing points. To begin, sight line intersections on PP in side view are projected to corresponding sight lines in top view, then to perspective view at proper height, taken off PP.

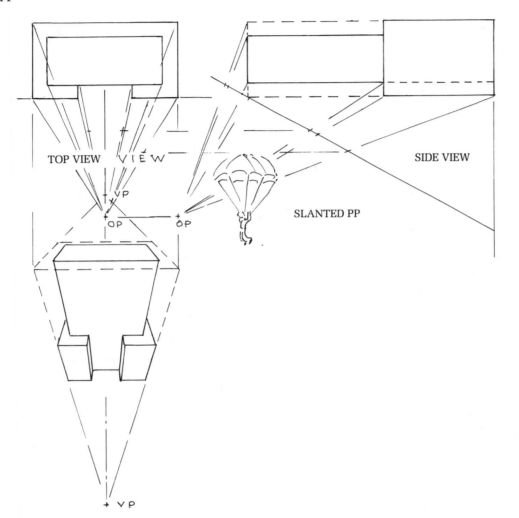

TOP VIEW   VIEW

SIDE VIEW

SLANTED PP

+ VP

+ OP   + OP

+ VP

SLANTED PICTURE PLANE
Close and high observation points. Side view
has been reversed to save space. Picture
plane is slanted backward. Since the object is
parallel to the picture plane there are only
two vanishing points, both vertical.

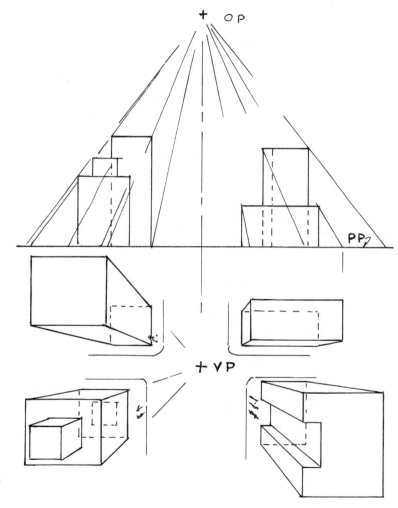

BIRD'S-EYE VIEW
*Picture plane is flat and observation point
extremely high. Sight lines of the top of each
object are projected onto PP. The diverging
lines of the various corners in the perspective
radiate from each base in the top view.*

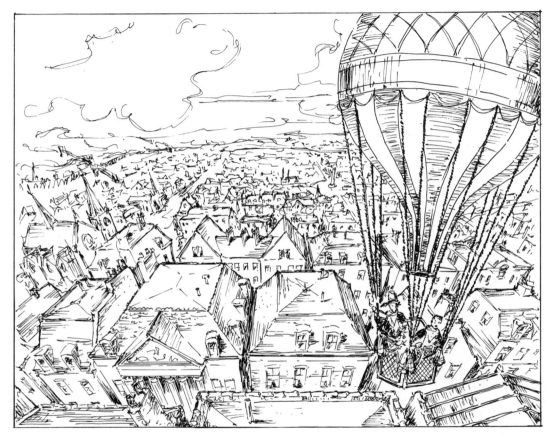

Sketch with very high horizon line. Note that the sides of buildings converge to a vertical vanishing point.

22

Problems

Problem 8. Perspective

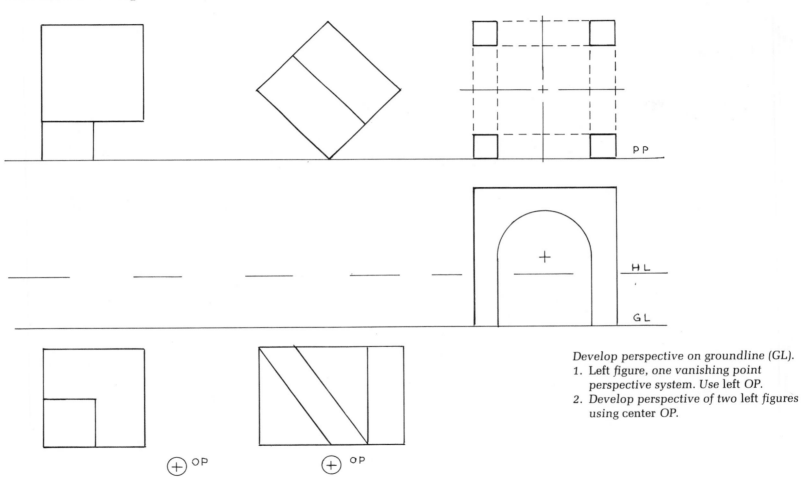

PP

HL

GL

Develop perspective on groundline (GL).
1. Left figure, one vanishing point perspective system. Use left OP.
2. Develop perspective of two left figures using center OP.

OP

OP

Problem 9. One Vanishing Point Perspective

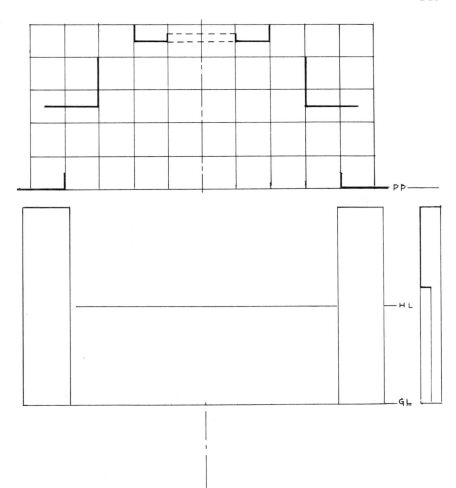

1. *Locate VP.*   2. *Develop perspective of floor grid.*

3. *Develop perspective of set. Scenery*

and door heights are to the right.

Problem 10. Perspective Grid Technique

Develop perspective of floor grid and setting. Heights of scenery, door and window opening right and left.

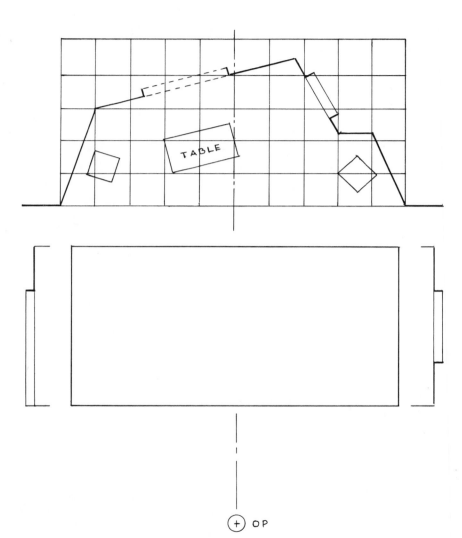